# THE
# BARD
# IN
# BRIEF

# SHAKESPEARE IN QUOTATIONS

SELECTED BY
HANNAH MANKTELOW

BRITISH LIBRARY

# CONTENTS

# SHAKESPEARE IN PRINT

T HE IDEA THAT HE WOULD ONE DAY SEE HIS WORKS IN PRINT
had probably never occurred to William Shakespeare when he set off
from Stratford-upon-Avon to pursue a theatrical career in London. Plays
were written for the stage rather than the page and, despite a flourishing
print industry, dramatic works made up just a small percentage of the wider
market. Shakespeare's success, however, defied convention. By the end of
his career, Shakespeare had become one of the most published authors ever:
during his lifetime all of his poems and about half of his plays appeared in
print; eighteen further pieces followed in the First Folio of 1623. As none of
his manuscripts survive, these early printed editions are the closest we can
come to Shakespeare's original texts.

Shakespeare himself had little to do with the printing of his plays. Like
most early modern playwrights, he was employed by a theatre company
and they retained the rights to all the work that he produced for them.
If they chose to sell a script to a printer – perhaps because the company
needed money or were disbanding – they would receive a one-off fee. Only
Shakespeare's early narrative poems *Venus and Adonis* (1593) and *The Rape
of Lucrece* (1594) appear to have been printed with his direct input. Both
feature a personal dedication to the Earl of Southampton, who may have
been Shakespeare's patron. The two poems became bestsellers, with each
appearing in multiple editions before Shakespeare's death in 1616. While
plays were generally considered ephemeral and of little artistic merit, poetry
was held in high regard. The astounding popularity of these works helped
to establish Shakespeare's reputation as a talented writer.

Prior to 1623, most of Shakespeare's plays and poems were printed in paperback quartos; one, a version of *Henry VI Part 3* (1595) was printed in octavo. In quarto publications a printed sheet was folded in half twice to give four leaves, and in the smaller octavo it was folded thrice, giving eight leaves. Quartos were usually sold for sixpence, which was about a third of a skilled labourer's daily wage, and six times as much as the cheapest theatre ticket. Although printed in London, copies were distributed by book-sellers throughout the country. Most were bought to be read for pleasure, while others were purchased by provincial players in order to stage their own productions of Shakespeare's works.

The quartos varied in quality. Some, such as *The Merchant of Venice* (1600) and *Much Ado About Nothing* (1600), appear to have been taken from authentic final texts. Others, including *King Richard III* (1597), *Troilus and Cressida* (1609), and *Othello* (1622), may have been from early drafts that Shakespeare later revised. Seven editions have been traditionally classified as 'bad' quartos: *The Taming of a Shrew* (1594); *The First Part of the Contention betwixt the two famous Houses of Yorke and Lancaster*, aka *King Henry VI, Part 2* (1594); *The true Tragedy of Richard Duke of York*, aka *King Henry VI, Part 3* (1595); *Romeo and Juliet* (1597); *King Henry V* (1600); *Sir John Falstaff*, aka *The Merry Wives of Windsor* (1602); and *Hamlet* (1603). These all differ significantly from later versions and feature major deviations in title, character, text, and plot. Perhaps the most notorious discrepancy is Hamlet's speech in the 1603 quarto, which begins, 'To be, or not to be, I there's the point'. For a long time scholars believed that these editions were assembled using the recollections of actors and audience members. More recently, it has been argued that the 'bad' quartos were either based on Shakespeare's rough drafts, known as 'foul papers', or that they were adaptations created to suit particular circumstances.

Seven years after Shakespeare's death, new versions of several quarto texts as well as previously unpublished pieces appeared together in a collected volume. 'Mr. William Shakespeares Comedies, Histories, & Tragedies', often referred to now as the First Folio, was conceived and executed by John Heminges and Henry Condell. As friends and former colleagues of Shakespeare, they had access to a wide range of manuscripts and spent years preparing what they hoped would become the authoritative edition of his plays. In their introduction, Heminges and Condell declared that the public had been 'abused with divers stolen and surreptitious copies, maimed and deformed by the frauds and stealths of injurious imposters', implying that the previously printed quartos were unauthorised. Their Folio was a carefully-produced luxury item, bound in calfskin and costing one pound – a sizeable sum of money.

The First Folio had an enduring impact on the printing and wider reception of Shakespeare's work. Not only was this the first time that his plays had been categorised into comedies, histories, and tragedies, but the pieces selected by Heminges and Condell have, with a few additions, formed the basis of the Shakespeare canon. *Pericles* (1607) and *The Two Noble Kinsmen* (1613) were excluded from the Folio but are now widely accepted as having been written by Shakespeare and a collaborator. Two more plays were attributed to Shakespeare in his lifetime but also failed to make it into the Folio: *Love's Labour's Won* (1595–96) and *Cardenio* (1612–13). Unlike the collaborative pieces, these were never printed, and appear to be lost for good.

The quotations in this collection have been selected from forty-five works of Shakespeare. Alongside the canonical plays are two narrative poems, a selection of sonnets, and two plays that have traditionally been classed as 'Apocrypha' – works of disputed authorship to which Shakespeare may have contributed. Touching on pivotal, revealing, or iconic moments in each piece, the quotations are illustrated from the earliest printed editions held by the British Library. The only exceptions to this are *Romeo and Juliet* and *King Henry VI, Part 2*, which do not feature the selected quotations in their first editions. The text, titles, and references for most of the plays and all the poems have been taken from the *Arden Shakespeare Complete Works* (2011); for the Apocrypha, the Royal Shakespeare Company's *William Shakespeare and Others: Collaborative Plays* (2013) has been used. Both editions regularise and modernise spelling and punctuation, and in those plays that were first printed in 'bad' quartos there may be considerable differences between the text and the illustration. Finally, the quotations appear in the order in which the editors of *The Oxford Shakespeare* (2005) believe they were written: from *The Two Gentlemen of Verona* (1589–91) to *The Two Noble Kinsmen* (1613).

Sweet Lady, entertaine him for your Seruant.

*Pro.* My dutie will I boaſt of, nothing elſe.

*Sil.* And dutie neuer yet did want his meed.
Seruant, you are welcome to a worthleſſe Miſtreſſe.

*Pro.* Ile die on him that ſaies ſo but your ſelfe.

*Sil.* That you are welcome?

*Pro.* That you are worthleſſe. (you.

*Thur.* Madam, my Lord your father wold ſpeak with

*Sil.* I wait vpon his pleaſure : Come Sir *Thurio*,
Goe with me : once more, new Seruant welcome ;
Ile leaue you to confer of home affaires,
When you haue done, we looke too heare from you.

*Pro.* Wee'll both attend vpon your Ladiſhip.

*Val.* Now tell me : how do al from whence you came?

*Pro.* Your frends are wel, & haue thē much cōmended.

*Val.* And how doe yours?

*Pro.* I left them all in health.

*Val.* How does your Lady? & how thriues your loue?

*Pro.* My tales of Loue were wont to weary you,
I know you ioy not in a Loue-diſcourſe.

*Val.* I *Protheus*, but that life is alter'd now,
I haue done pennance for contemning Loue,
Whoſe high emperious thoughts haue puniſh'd me
With bitter faſts, with penitentiall grones,
With nightly teares, and daily hart-ſore ſighes,
For in reuenge of my contempt of loue,
Loue hath chas'd ſleepe from my enthralled eyes,
And made them watchers of mine owne hearts ſorrow.
O gentle *Protheus*, Loue's a mighty Lord,

The wate
Forgiue
Becauſe t
My fooli
(Onely fo
Is gone w
For Loue

*Pro.* B

*Val.* I,
With all t
Determin
The Ladd
Plotted, a
Good *Pro*
In theſe af

*Pro.* C
I muſt vnt
Some nece
And then

*Val.* V

*Pro.* I
Euen as or
Or as one
So the rem
Is by a nev
It is mine,
Her true p
That make
Shee is fai

# THE TWO GENTLEMEN OF VERONA

## Act 2, Scene 4

**Valentine:** I have done penance for contemning Love,
Whose high imperious thoughts have punish'd me
With bitter fasts, with penitential groans,
With nightly tears, and daily heart-sore sighs,
For in revenge of my contempt of Love,
Love hath chas'd sleep from my enthralled eyes,
And made them watchers of mine own heart's sorrow.

**Context:** Adventurous Valentine has left Verona for Milan, scornful of his friend Proteus's decision to stay at home in the hope of winning Julia's heart. Just as she reciprocates his affections the lovers are separated, and Proteus is sent to Milan by his father. Upon his arrival, Valentine reveals that he has fallen desperately in love with the Duke's daughter Sylvia, and regrets his earlier dismissal of romance.

**Dates:** The first mention of *The Two Gentlemen of Verona* was made in 1598, but many believe it was written much earlier, between 1589 and 1591. It is believed to have been the first play that Shakespeare wrote for the London stage, and was originally published in the First Folio of 1623.

**Image:** *First Folio, 1623.*

*Gree.* And *Michael*, you ſhall beare no newes of this tide.
Becauſe they two may be in Rainam down before your M.
   *Mich.* Why, Ile agree to any thing you'l haue me.
So you will accept of my companie.     *Exeunt.*

      *Here enters Mosbie.*

   *Mosb.* Diſturbed thoughts driues me from company,
And dries my marrow with their watchfulnes,
Continuall trouble of my moody braine,
Feebles my body by exceſſe of drinke,
And nips me, as the bitter Northeaſt wind
Doth checke the tender bloſſoms in the Spring.
Well-fares the man how ere his cates doe taſte,
That tables not with foule ſuſpition :
And he but pines amongſt his delicates,
Whoſe troubled mind is ſtuft with diſcontent.
My golden time was when I had no gold,
Though then I wanted, yet I ſlept ſecure,
My daily toile, begat me nights repoſe :
My nights repoſe made day-light freſh to me.
But ſince I climb'd the top bough of the tree,
And ſought to build my neſt among the clouds,
Each gentle ſtary gaile doth ſhake my bed :
And makes me dread my downefall to the earth,
But whither doth contemplation carry me.
The way I ſeeke to finde, where pleaſure dwels,
Is hedged behind me, that I cannot backe,
But needs muſt on, although to dangers gate :
Then *Arden* periſh thou by that decree.
For *Greene* doth heyre the land and weed thee vp,

                                                    To

# ARDEN OF FAVERSHAM

## Scene 8

**Mosby:** My golden time was when I had no gold.
Though then I wanted, yet I slept secure:
My daily toil begat me night's repose,
My night's repose made daylight fresh to me.
But since I climbed the top bough of the tree
And sought to build my nest among the clouds,
Each gentle starry gale doth shake my bed
And makes me dread my downfall to the earth.

**Context:** Ruthless landowner Thomas Arden has made many enemies in Faversham, not least his young wife Alice. When he acquires a valuable lot of land belonging to a former abbey, Alice and her lover Mosby plot to see Arden dead. Their first attempts have ended in failure, and in this scene Mosby reflects on their actions and the turmoil he has experienced since his rise from commoner to steward.

**Dates:** *Arden of Faversham* was based on real events that took place in February 1551. The play was probably written around 1590 and was first printed in quarto in 1592. Some scholars believe that Shakespeare wrote all or part of the play; scene 8 is considered the most likely section. Thomas Kyd and Christopher Marlowe have also been suggested as authors, while others have argued it is the work of an unknown amateur.

**Image:** *Third Quarto, 1633.*

It shall be moone, or starre, or what I list,
Or ere I iourney to your Fathers house :
Goe on, and fetch our horses backe againe,
Euermore croft and croft, nothing but croft.

    *Hort.* Say as he saies, or we shall neuer goe.

    *Kate.* Forward I pray, since we haue come so farre,
And be it moone, or sunne, or what you please :
And if you please to call it a rush Candle,
Henceforth I vowe it shall be so for me.

    *Petr.* I say it is the Moone.

    *Kate.* I know it is the Moone.

    *Petr.* Nay then you lye : it is the blessed Sunne.

    *Kate.* Then God be blest, it in the blessed sun,
But sunne it is not, when you say it is not,
And the Moone changes euen as your minde :
What you will haue it nam'd, euen that it is,
And so it shall be so for *Katherine.*

    *Hort.* Petruchio, goe thy waies, the field is won.

    *Petr.* Well, forward, forward, thus the bowle should
And not vnluckily against the Bias :    (run,
But soft, Company is comming here.

*Enter Vincentio.*

Good morrow gentle Mistris, where away :
Tell me sweete *Kate,* and tell me truely too,
Hast thou beheld a fresher Gentlewoman :
Such warre of white and red within her cheekes :
What stars do spangle heauen with such beautie,
As those two eyes become that heauenly face ?
Faire louely Maide, once more good day to thee :
Sweete *Kate* embrace her for her beauties sake.

    *Hort.* A will make the man mad to make the woman
of him.

    *Kate.* Yong budding Virgin, faire, and fresh, & sweet,
Whether away, or whether is thy aboade ?
Happy the Parents of so faire a childe ;
Happier the man whom fauourable stars

And wander we to see t
Who will of thy arriual

    *Vinc.* But is this true
Like pleasant trauailors
Vpon the companie you

    *Hort.* I doe assure th

    *Petr.* Come goe ale
For our first merriment

    *Hor.* Well Petruchi
Haue to my Widdow,
Then hast thou taught

*Enter Biondello, L*
is

    *Biond.* Softly and sw

    *Luc.* I flie *Biondello* ;
thee at home, therefore

    *Biond.* Nay faith, I
and then come backe to

    *Gre.* I maruaile *Car*

*Enter Petruchio,*
with

    *Petr.* Sir heres the d
My Fathers beares mor
Thither must I, and here

    *Vin.* You shall not c
I thinke I shall comman
And by all likelihood s

    *Grem.* They're busi
lowder.

    *Pedant looke*

    *Ped.* What's he that
the gate?

    *Vin.* Is Signior *Luce*

    *Ped.* He's within sir
    *Vinc.* What if a ma

# THE TAMING OF THE SHREW

## Act 4, Scene 5

**Katherina:** Then, God be blest, it is the blessed sun.
But sun it is not, when you say it is not,
And the moon changes even as your mind.
What you will have it nam'd, even that it is,
And so it shall be so for Katherine.

**Context:** To the despair of her numerous suitors, sweet Bianca is unable to marry until her older sister, the shrewish Katherina, is wed. When Petruchio arrives in Padua he soon hears of Katherina's sizable dowry and, undaunted by her fierce temper, is determined to make her his wife. Immediately after their wedding Petruchio takes Katherina back to his house, where he sets about breaking her spirit. Here, a sleep-deprived and starving Katherina succumbs to Petruchio's will and agrees to accept his version of reality, whatever that may be.

**Dates:** *The Taming of the Shrew* was probably written between 1589 and 1591 and was first printed in the First Folio of 1623. In 1594 a play named *The Taming of a Shrew* was published in quarto; this may have been Shakespeare's original source, an alternative version, or an earlier draft of the same piece.

e ask'd herein before?

will be there.

d Mafter Sherife,

the Kings Commiffion.

here my Commiffion ftayes:

ated now,

le of Man.

rotect my Lady here?

charge, may't pleafe your

worfe, in that I pray

may laugh againe,

rdneffe, if you doe it her.

Lord, and bid me not fare-

, I cannot ftay to fpeake.

*Exit Glofter.*

all comfort goe with thee,

y Ioy, is Death;

haue beene afear'd,

s eternitie.

ke me hence,

e no fauor;

u art commanded.

hat is to the Ile of Man,

o your State.

gh, for I am but reproach:

oachfully?

, and Duke *Hunfreyes* Lady,

fhall be vs'd.

nd better then I fare,

onduct of my fhame.

d Madame pardon me.

Office is difcharg'd;

nance done,

our Iourney.

And *Humfrey* is no little Man in England.
Firft note, that he is neere you in difcent,
And fhould you fall, he is the next will mount.
Me feemeth then, it is no Pollicie,
Refpecting what a rancorous minde he beares,
And his aduantage following your deceafe,
That he fhould come about your Royall Perfon,
Or be admitted to your Highneffe Councell.
By flatterie hath he wonne the Commons hearts :
And when he pleafe to make Commotion,
'Tis to be fear'd they all will follow him.
Now 'tis the Spring, and Weeds are fhallow-rooted,
Suffer them now, and they'le o're-grow the Garden,
And choake the Herbes for want of Husbandry.
The reuerent care I beare vnto my Lord,
Made me collect thefe dangers in the Duke.
If it be fond, call it a Womans feare:
Which feare, if better Reafons can fupplant,
I will fubfcribe, and fay I wrong'd the Duke.
My Lord of Suffolke, Buckingham, and Yorke,
Reproue my allegation, if you can,
Or elfe conclude my words effectuall.

*Suff.* Well hath your Highneffe feene into this Duke:
And had I firft beene put to fpeake my minde,
I thinke I fhould haue told your Graces Tale.
The Ducheffe, by his fubornation,
Vpon my Life began her diuellifh practifes :
Or if he were not priuie to thofe Faults,
Yet by reputing of his high difcent,
As next the King, he was fucceffiue Heire,
And fuch high vaunts of his Nobilitie,
Did inftigate the Bedlam braine-ficke Ducheffe,
By wicked meanes to frame our Soueraignes fall.
Smooth runnes the Water, where the Brooke is deepe,
And in his fimple fhew he harbours Treafon.
The Fox barkes not, when he would fteale the Lambe.
No, no, my Soueraigne, *Glouster* is a man
Vnfounded yet, and full of deepe deceit.

*Card.* Did he not, contrary to forme of Law,

# KING HENRY VI, PART 2
## Act 3, Scene 1

**Queen Margaret:** By flattery hath he won the commons' hearts;
And when he please to make commotion,
'Tis to be feared they all will follow him.
Now 'tis the spring, and weeds are shallow-rooted;
Suffer them now and they'll o'ergrow the garden
And choke the herbs for want of husbandry.
The reverent care I bear unto my lord
Made me collect these dangers in the Duke.

**Context:** England and France have made a fragile peace, but Henry VI must now face the discord of his own court. He has recently married the French princess Margaret against the wishes of his uncle and Protector, the Duke of Gloucester. Together the new Queen Margaret, her lover the Duke of Suffolk, and Richard Duke of York, a pretender to the throne, plot to bring down Gloucester. They banish his wife Eleanor and then, in this scene, feign concern that Gloucester may harbour ambitions for the crown.

**Dates:** *Henry VI, Part 2* was probably written between 1590 and 1591. It was first published in quarto in 1594 as *The First Part of the Contention betwixt the two famous Houses of Yorke and Lancaster, with the death of the good Duke Humphrey: And the banishment and death of the Duke of Suffolke, and the Tragicall end of the proud Cardinall of Winchester, with the notable Rebellion of Iacke Cade: And the Duke of Yorkes first claime vnto the Crowne.* The quarto text differs considerably from the better-known version printed in the First Folio of 1623.

O God forgiue my sinnes, and pardon thee.        *He*

    *Glo.* What? will the aspyring blood of *Lancaster*
Sinke into the ground? I had thought it would haue mou
See how my sword weepes for the poore Kings death,
Now may such purple teares be alwayes shed,
For such as seeke the downefall of our house,
If any sparke of life remaine in thee,

                        *Stabbe him againe.*
Downe, downe to hell, and say I sent thee thither,
I that haue neither pittie, loue, nor feare:
Indeed twas true that *Henrie* tolde me of,
For I haue often heard my mother say,
That I came into the worlde with my legges forward:
And had I not reason thinke you to make haste,
And seeke their ruines that vsurpt our rights?
The women wept, and the Midwife cride,
O Iesus blesse vs, he is borne with teeth,
And so I was indeed : which plainely signifide,
That I should snarle and bite, and play the dogge.
Then since Heauen hath made my body so,
Let Hell make crookt my minde, to answere it.
I had no father; I am like no father.
I haue no brother; I am like no brothers.

# KING HENRY VI, PART 3

## Act 5, Scene 6

**Richard, Duke of Gloucester:**

The midwife wonder'd, and the women cried
'O Jesu bless us, he is born with teeth!'
And so I was, which plainly signified
That I should snarl, and bite, and play the dog.
Then, since the heavens have shap'd my body so,
Let hell make crook'd my mind to answer it.

**Context:** England is in the midst of a bloody civil war between the Yorkists and Lancastrians. Richard, Duke of York has been murdered by Queen Margaret's forces and his three sons are at odds with one another. Clarence has revolted against Edward and Richard, Duke of Gloucester (soon to be Richard III), but is reconciled when Edward achieves a definitive victory and is crowned king. As the defeated Margaret is imprisoned and her young son murdered, Richard slips away to kill Henry, revealing his villainous self-interest in a soliloquy.

**Dates:** *Henry VI, Part 3* was probably written immediately after *Part 2,* in 1591. In 1595 a version of the play was printed in octavo as *The true Tragedie of Richard Duke of Yorke, and the death of good King Henrie the Sixt.* A second quarto edition was printed in 1600, which used a similar but not identical text to the octavo. There are substantial differences between these earlier texts and that of the First Folio of 1623; the octavo version may have been an early draft or created for a smaller playing company.

**Image:** *Second Quarto, 1600.*

*Talb.* Where is my other Life? mine owne is gone.
O, where's young *Talbot*? where is valiant *Iohn*?
Triumphant Death, fmear'd with Captiuitie,
Young *Talbots* Valour makes me fmile at thee.
When he perceiu'd me fhrinke, and on my Knee,
His bloodie Sword he brandifht ouer mee,
And like a hungry Lyon did commence
Rough deeds of Rage, and fterne Impatience:
But when my angry Guardant ftood alone,
Tendring my ruine, and affayl'd of none,
Dizzie-ey'd Furie, and great rage of Heart,
Suddenly made him from my fide to ftart
Into the cluftring Battaile of the French:
And in that Sea of Blood, my Boy did drench
His ouer-mounting Spirit; and there di'de
My *Icarus*, my Bloffome, in his pride.

*Enter with Iohn Talbot, borne.*
*Seru.* O my deare Lord, loe where your Sonne is borr
*Tal.* Thou antique Death, which laugh'ft vs here tc fcor
Anon from thy infulting Tyrannie,
Coupled in bonds of perpetuitie,
Two *Talbots* winged through the lither Skie,
In thy defpight fhall fcape Mortalitie.

# KING HENRY VI, PART 1
## Act 4, Scene 7

**Talbot:** But when my angry guardant stood alone,
Tendering my ruin and assailed of none,
Dizzy-eyed fury and great rage of heart
Suddenly made him from my side to start
Into the clustering battle of the French,
And in that sea of blood my boy did drench
His over-mounting spirit, and there died
My Icarus, my blossom, in his pride.

**Context:** Henry V has been succeeded by the young Henry VI, who rules under the protectorship of his uncles Gloucester and Exeter. War with France rages on, while at home the Houses of York and Lancaster are increasingly divided. In this speech the valiant English commander, Sir John Talbot, describes the death of his son at the disastrous siege of Bordeaux.

**Dates:** *The First Part of Henry the Sixth* is believed to have been written after parts 2 and 3, and has been dated to 1592. The play appears to be a collaborative work between Shakespeare and two or three other writers; Thomas Nashe is the likely author of Act 1. It was originally published in the First Folio of 1623.

I should be Author to dishonour you,
But on mine honour dare I vndertake,
For good Lord *Titus* innocence in all :
Whose fury not dissembled speakes his griefes :
Then at my sute looke gracioufly on him,
Loose not so noble a friend on vaine suppose,
Nor with sowre lookes afflict his gentle heart.

My Lord, be ruld by me, be wonne at last,
Dissemble all your griefes and discontents,
You are but newly planted in your Throne,
Least then the people, and Patricians too,
Vpon a iust suruay take *Titus* part,
And so supplant vs for ingratude,
Which Rome reputes to be a hainous sinne.
Yeeld at intreats, and then let me alone
Ile finde a day to massacre them all,
And race their faction and their familie,
The cruell Father, and his traytrous sonnes,
To whome I sued for my deere sonnes life.

C.

And

*The most lamentable Tragedie*

And make them know what tis to let a Queene
Kneele in the streetes, and beg for grace in vaine.
Come, come, sweet Emperour, (come *Andronicus* )
Take vp this good old man, and cheere the heart,
That dies in tempest of thy angry frowne.

*King.* Rise *Titus*, rise, my Empresse hath preuaild.
*Titus.* I thanke your maiestie, and her my Lord.
These words, these lookes, infuse new life in me.
*Tamora.* *Titus* I am incorporate in Rome,

# TITUS ANDRONICUS

## Act 1, Scene 1

**Tamora:** My lord, be ruled by me, be won at last,
Dissemble all your griefs and discontents.
You are but newly planted in your throne;
Lest then the people, and patricians too,
Upon a just survey take Titus' part,
And so supplant you for ingratitude,
Which Rome reputes to be a heinous sin,
Yield at entreats – and then let me alone:
I'll find a day to massacre them all,
And raze their faction and their family,
The cruel father and his traitorous sons
To whom I sued for my dear son's life,
And make them know what 'tis to let a queen
Kneel in the streets and beg for grace in vain.

**Context:** Tamora, Queen of the Goths, has been captured by the Roman general Titus Andronicus and paraded through the streets. Despite her pleas, Titus publically sacrifices the eldest of her three remaining sons. The newly elected Roman emperor Saturninus offers to marry Lavinia, daughter of Titus, but she has promised herself to his brother Bassianus, with whom she promptly escapes. Humiliated, Saturninus instead weds Tamora, who swears that if he follows her she will take bloody revenge on Titus and his kin for both their sakes.

**Dates:** Recent scholarship suggests that *The Most Lamentable Romaine Tragedie of Titus Andronicus* was written in 1592. The play's first recorded performance was in January 1594 at the Rose playhouse, and it was published later that same year. The first of Shakespeare's plays to appear in print, *Titus Andronicus* was almost certainly the product of some sort of collaboration with George Peele.

**Image:** *Third Quarto, 1611.*

I that am rudely ſtampt and want loues maieſty,
To ſtrut before a wanton ambling Nymph:
I that am curtaild of this faire proportion,
Cheated of feature by diſſembling nature,
Deformd, vnfiniſht, ſent before my time
Into this breathing world ſcarce halfe made vp,
And that ſo lamely and vnfaſhionable,
That dogs barke at me as I halt by them:
Why I in this weake piping time of peace
Haue no delight to paſſe away the time,
Vnleſſe to ſpie my ſhadow in the ſunne,
And deſcant on mine owne deformity:
And therefore ſince I cannot prooue a louer
To entertaine theſe faire well ſpoken daies,

## The Tragedy

I am determined to prooue a villaine,
And hate the idle pleaſures of theſe daies:
Plots haue I laid inductious dangerous,
By drunken Propheſies, libels and dreames,
To ſet my brother Clarence and the King
In deadly hate the one againſt the other.
And if King Edward be as true and iuſt,
As I am ſubtile, falſe, and trecherous:
This day ſhould Clarence cloſely be mewed vp,

# KING RICHARD III

## Act 1, Scene 1

**Richard:** I, that am curtail'd of this fair proportion,
Cheated of feature by dissembling Nature,
Deform'd, unfinish'd, sent before my time
Into this breathing world scarce half made up –
And that so lamely and unfashionable
That dogs bark at me, as I halt by them –
Why, I, in this weak piping time of peace,
Have no delight to pass away the time,
Unless to spy my shadow in the sun,
And descant on mine own deformity.
And therefore, since I cannot prove a lover
To entertain these fair well-spoken days,
I am determined to prove a villain,
And hate the idle pleasures of these days.

**Context:** Richard, Duke of Gloucester, is brother to Edward, the newly crowned King of England. In this opening speech, the first of many soliloquies, he rails against his physical deformity and makes it clear that what will follow – the murder of his brother and nephews, and eventual civil war against the Rivers – is born from his villainous nature, which allows him no enjoyment of peace or prosperity.

**Dates:** *King Richard III* is likely to have been written between 1592 and 1593. In tone as well as narrative sequence it acts as a sequel to *Henry VI, Part 3*. The play was first published in quarto in 1597 with a plot-spoiling title: *The Tragedy of King Richard the third. Containing, His treacherous Plots against his brother Clarence: the pittiefull murther of his innocent nephewes: his tyrannicall vsurpation: with the whole course of his detested life, and most deserued death.*

**Image:** *First Quarto, 1597.*

Now quicke defire hath caught the yeelding pray,
And gluttonlike she feeds, yet neuer filleth,
Her lips are conquerers, his lips obay,
Paying what ranfome the infulter willeth :
  VVhofe vultur thought doth pitch the price fo hie,
  That she will draw his lips rich treafure drie.

And hauing felt the fweetneffe of the fpoile,
VVith blindfold fury she begins to forrage,
Her face doth reeke, & fmoke, her blood doth boile,
And careleffe luft ftirs vp a defperate courage,
  Planting obliuion, beating reafon backe,
  Forgetting shames pure blush, & honors wracke.

Hot, faint, and wearie, with her hard imbracing,
Like a wild bird being tam'd with too much hādling,
Or as the fleet-foot Roe that's tyr'd with chafing,
Or like the froward infant ftild with dandling :
  He now obayes, and now no more refifteth,
  VVhile she takes all she can, not all she lifteth.

VVhat waxe fo frozen but diffolues with tempring,

# VENUS AND ADONIS

## Lines 547–552

Now quick desire hath caught the yielding prey,
And glutton-like she feeds, yet never filleth.
Her lips are conquerors, his lips obey,
Paying what ransom the insulter willeth;
      Whose vulture thought doth pitch the price so high
      That she will draw his lips' rich treasure dry.

**Context:** The goddess Venus is besotted by a beautiful youth named
Adonis and pursues him while he hunts in the forest. In a comic reversal
of gender roles he resists her attempts at seduction, forcing her to become
the hunter and he the prey. In this passage, Venus's frustration has caused
her to faint, and Adonis is compelled to revive her with a kiss. The goddess
enthusiastically takes advantage of their physical contact.

**Dates:** In 1592 an outbreak of plague throughout London caused the city
authorities to close all public playhouses. Shakespeare turned instead to
writing narrative poems, the first of which was *Venus and Adonis*. Published
in quarto in 1593, this was the first of Shakespeare's works to be printed
under his name and was the most successful in his own lifetime: it was
reprinted six times by 1600, and had undergone sixteen editions by 1640.

**Image:** *Second Quarto, 1594.*

Thus ebs and flowes the currant of her sorrow,
And time doth wearie time with her complayning,
Shee looks for night, & then shee longs for morrow,
And both shee thinks too long with her remayning.
Short time seems long, in sorrowes sharp sustayning,
   Though wo be heauie, yet it seldome sleepes,
   And they that watch, see time, how slow it creeps.

VVhich all this time hath ouerslipt her thought,
That shee with painted Images hath spent,
Being from the feeling of her own griefe brought,
By deepe surmise of others detriment,
Loosing her woes in shews of discontent :
   It easeth some, though none it euer cured,
   To thinke their dolour others haue endured.

But now the mindfull Messenger come backe,
Brings home his Lord and other companie,
VVho finds his LVCRECE clad in mourning black,
And round about her teare-distained eye
Blew circles stream'd, like Rain-bows in the skie.
   These watergalls in her dim Element,

# THE RAPE OF LUCRECE
## Lines 1569–1575

Thus ebbs and flows the current of her sorrow,
And time doth weary time with her complaining.
She looks for night, and then she longs for morrow,
And both she thinks too long with her remaining.
Short time seems long in sorrow's sharp sustaining:
      Though woe be heavy, yet it seldom sleeps,
      And they that watch see time how slow it creeps.

**Context:** Hearing Roman general Collatine praising his wife Lucrece's chastity and beauty, Tarquin, son of the Roman king, is compelled by his lust to visit her at her home in Collatium. He struggles with his conscience but eventually gags and rapes Lucrece before fleeing. Once alone, she is left to contemplate her ordeal, full of dread and yearning for the coming dawn.

**Dates:** *The Rape of Lucrece* was published in quarto in the summer of 1594 and was probably written earlier that year, as a follow-up to *Venus and Adonis*. Though it did not match the success of the earlier poem, *Lucrece* was another bestseller. It underwent nine editions by 1655, six of which appeared before Shakespeare's death in 1616.

**Image:** *First Quarto, 1594.*

*Pr.*How confident their ſtrength and number makes them,
Now *Audley* ſound thoſe ſiluer winges of thine,
And let thoſe milke white meſſengers of time,
Shew thy times learning in this dangerous time,
Thy ſelfe art buſie, and bit with many broiles,
And ſtratagems forepaſt with yron pens,
Are texted in thine honorable face,
Thou art a married man in this diſtreſſe,
But danger wooes me as a bluſhing maide,
Teach me an anſwere to this perillous time.

*Aud.*To die is all as common as to liue,
The one in choice the other holds in chaſe,
For from the inſtant we begin to liue,
We do purſue and hunt the time to die,
Firſt bud we,then we blow,and after ſeed,
Then preſently we fall,and as a ſhade
Followes the bodie,ſo we follow death,
If then we hunt for death,why do we feare it?
If we feare it,why do we follow it?
If we do feare,how can we ſhun it?
If we do feare,with feare we do but aide
The thing we feare,to ſeize on vs the ſooner,
If wee feare not,then no reſolued proffer,
Can ouerthrow the limit of our fate,
For whether ripe or rotten,drop we ſhall,
as we do drawe the lotterie of our doome.

*Pri.*Ah good olde man,a thouſand thouſand armors,
Theſe wordes of thine haue buckled on my backe,
Ah what an idiot haſt thou made of lyfe,
To ſeeke the thing it feares,and how diſgraſt,

# EDWARD III

## Act 4, Scene 4

**Lord Audley:** To die is all as common as to live:
The one enchased, the other holds in chase:
For from the instant we begin to live,
We do pursue and hunt the time to die.
First bud we, then we blow, and after seed,
Then presently we fall, and as a shade
Follows the body, so we follow death.
If then we hunt for death, why do we fear it?
If we fear it, why do we follow it?
If we do fear, how can we shun it?
If we do fear, with fear we do but aid
The thing we fear to seize on us the sooner.
If we fear not, then no resolvèd proffer
Can overthrow the limit of our fate:
For whether ripe or rotten, drop we shall,
As we do draw the lottery of our doom.

**Context:** After he is informed that he is the rightful heir to the recently deceased King of France, Edward III of England sets out to claim the throne. Following a series of triumphs against the Scots and the French, Edward III and his son, Prince Edward, force the French into retreat. The Prince is sent to Poitiers to pursue them, but seemingly faces disaster when he is surrounded on all sides. Here, battle-hardened Lord Audley makes a rousing speech that spurs the Prince on to eventual victory.

**Dates:** *The Raigne of King Edward the Third* was probably written between 1593 and 1594, and was published in quarto in 1596. Most scholars agree that Shakespeare wrote a handful of scenes; his collaborator is unknown, but the most likely candidates are George Peele, Christopher Marlowe, or Thomas Kyd.

**Image:** *First Quarto, 1596.*

What will you walke with me about the towne,
And then goe to my Inne and dine with me?

*E.Mar.* I am inuited fir to certaine Marchants,
Of whom I hope to make much benefit :
I craue your pardon, foone at fiue a clocke,
Pleafe you, Ile meete with you vpon the Mart,
And afterward confort you till bed time :
My prefent bufineffe cals me from you now.

*Ant.* Farewell till then : I will goe loofe my felfe,
And wander vp and downe to view the Citie.

*E.Mar.* Sir, I commend you to your owne content.

Exeunt.

*Ant.* He that commends me to mine owne content,
Commends me to the thing I cannot get :
I to the world am like a drop of water,
That in the Ocean feekes another drop,
Who falling there to finde his fellow forth,
(Vnfeene, inquifitiue) confounds himfelfe.
So I, to finde a Mother and a Brother,
In queft of them (vnhappie a) loofe my felfe.

*Enter Dromio of Ephefus.*

Here comes the almanacke of my true date :
What now ? How chance thou art return'd fo foone.

*E.Dro.* Return'd fo foone, rather approacht too late:
The Capon burnes, the Pig fals from the fpit;
The clocke hath ftrucken twelue vpon the bell :
My Miftris made it one vpon my cheeke :
She is fo hot becaufe the meate is colde :
The meate is colde, becaufe you come not home:
You come not home, becaufe you haue no ftomacke :
You haue no ftomacke, hauing broke your faft :
But we that know what 'tis to faft and pray,
Are penitent for your default to day.

*Ant.* Stop in your winde fir, tell me this I pray ?

# THE COMEDY OF ERRORS
## Act 1, Scene 2

**Antipholus of Syracuse:** He that commends me to mine own content
Commends me to the thing I cannot get.
I to the world am like a drop of water
That in the ocean seeks another drop,
Who, falling there to find his fellow forth,
(Unseen, inquisitive) confounds himself.
So I, to find a mother and a brother,
In quest of them, unhappy, lose myself.

**Context:** The cities of Syracuse and Ephesus are at war. Egeon, an elderly Syracusan, has been arrested for his trespass in Ephesus. He explains that many years ago he, his wife, their twin sons, and twin servants were in a shipwreck that cleaved the family in two. His son, Antipholus, has come to Ephesus in search of his missing brother, accompanied by his servant Dromio; their twin counterparts share the same names. Here, Antipholus of Syracuse speaks of the grief he has felt since the familial separation.

**Dates:** The first recorded performance of *The Comedy of Errors* appears to have been at Gray's Inn, a London law school, in December 1594. It may have been specially composed for the occasion. The play was originally published in the First Folio of 1623.

Consider what you first did sweare vnto:
To fast, to study, and to see no woman:
Flat treason gainst the kingly state of youth,
Say, Can you fast? your stomacks are too young:
And abstinence ingenders maladies.
And where that you haue vowd to studie (Lordes)
In that each of you haue forsworne his Booke.
Can you still dreame and poare and thereon looke.
For when would you my Lord, or you, or you,
Haue found the ground of Studies excellence,
Without the beautie of a womans face?
From womens eyes this doctrine I deriue,
They are the Ground, the Bookes, the Achadems,
From whence doth spring the true *Promethean* fire.
Why vniuersall plodding poysons vp
The nimble spirites in the arteries,
As motion and long during action tyres
The sinnowy vigour of the trauayler.
Now for not looking on a womans face,
You haue in that forsworne the vse of eyes:
And studie too, the causer of your vow.
For where is any Authour in the worlde,
Teaches such beautie as a womas eye:
Learning is but an adiunct to our selfe,
And where we are, our Learning likewise is.
Then when our selues we see in Ladies eyes,
With our selues,
Do we not likewise see our learning there?

# LOVE'S LABOUR'S LOST

## Act 4, Scene 3

**Berowne:** Consider what you first did swear unto:
To fast, to study, and to see no woman–
Flat treason 'gainst the kingly state of youth.
Say, can you fast? Your stomachs are too young,
And abstinence engenders maladies.

**Context:** The King of Navarre and his reluctant companions have sworn to devote themselves to study and to avoid women for three years. When the Princess of France and her ladies arrive on a diplomatic visit, the King is forced to accommodate them. The young men struggle, and ultimately fail, to keep their vows. Here the witty Berowne makes excuses for their conduct.

**Dates:** *Love's Labour's Lost* is usually dated to 1594 or 1595. It was performed at court for Queen Elizabeth I in 1596 or 1597, and first published in quarto in 1598. In following years Shakespeare wrote another play titled *Love's Labour's Won*, which may have served as a sequel. Contemporary records suggest this was performed and printed before 1603, but neither text nor plot have survived.

**Image:** *First Quarto, 1598.*

Where will doth mutiny with wits regard:
Direct not him whose way himselfe wil chuse.
Tis breath thou lackst, and that breath wilt thou loose:

Gaunt Me thinkes I am a prophet new inspirde,
And thus expiring do foretell of him,
His rash fierce blaze of ryot cannot last:
For violent fires soone burne out themselues.
Small showres last long, but sodaine stormes are short:
He tires betimes that spurs too fast betimes
With eagre feeding foode doth choke the feeder,
Light vanitie insatiate cormorant,
Consuming meanes soone praies vpon it selfe:
This royall throne of Kings, this sceptred Ile,
This earth of maiestie, this seate of Mars,
This other Eden, demy Paradice,
This fortresse built by Nature for her selfe,
Against infection and the hand of warre,
This happy breede of men, this little world,
This precious stone set in the siluer sea,
Which serues it in the office of a wall,
Or as moate defensiue to a house,
Against the enuie of lesse happier lands.
This blessed plot, this earth, this realme, this England,
This nurse, this teeming wombe of royall Kings,
Feard by their breed, and famous by theyr byrth,
Renowned for theyr deedes as far from home,
For christian seruice, and true chiualry,

# KING RICHARD II

## Act 2, Scene 1

**John of Gaunt:** This happy breed of men, this little world,
This precious stone set in the silver sea,
Which serves it in the office of a wall,
Or as a moat defensive to a house,
Against the envy of less happier lands;
This blessed plot, this earth, this realm, this England,

**Context:** King Richard II is a greedy and ineffective king, disliked for his excessive lifestyle and questionable advisors. He interrupts a dual between two men, Henry Bolingbroke and Thomas Mowbray, who have each accused the other of the murder of the Duke of Gloucester. Rather than allow the combat to continue, Richard banishes them both, drawing suspicion that he himself may be implicated in the crime. In this scene the elderly John of Gaunt, father to Bolingbroke and uncle to Richard, is sick and dying. He decries his nephew's ineffective reign and speaks lovingly of the realm of England.

**Dates:** *The Tragedie of King Richard the second* was probably written about 1595, and was first published in quarto in 1597. In 1608, a new quarto edition featured a scene depicting Richard's deposition. This may have been removed from earlier performances and printings due to its political content: such material could have been considered inflammatory during the reign of Queen Elizabeth I who, like Richard II, was notorious for promoting her favourites. The new material appeared in the First Folio of 1623.

**Image:** *First Quarto, 1597.*

That runnawayes eyes may wincke, and *Romeo*
Leape to these armes, vntalkt of and vnseene,
Louers can see to do their amorous rights,
And by their owne bewties, or if loue be blind,
It best agrees with night, come ciuill night,
Thou sober suted matron all in blacke,
And learne me how to loose a winning match,
Plaide for a paire of stainlesse maydenhoods.
Hood my vnmand bloud bayting in my cheekes,
With thy blacke mantle, till strange loue grow bold,
Thinke true loue acted simple modestie:
Come night, come *Romeo*, come thou day in night,
For thou wilt lie vpon the winges of night,
Whiter then new snow vpon a Rauens backe:
Come gentle night, come louing black browd night,
Giue me my *Romeo*, and when I shall die,
Take him and cut him out in little starres,
And he will make the face of heauen so fine,
That all the world will be in loue with night,
And pay no worship to the garish Sun.
O I haue bought the mansion of a loue,
But not possest it, and though I am sold,
Not yet enioyd, so tedious is this day,
As is the night before some festiuall,
To an impatient child that hath new robes
And may not weare them. O here comes my Nurse.

*Enter Nurse with cordes.*

# ROMEO AND JULIET

## Act 3, Scene 2

**Juliet:** Come night, come Romeo, come thou day in night,
For thou wilt lie upon the wings of night
Whiter than new snow upon a raven's back.
Come gentle night, come loving black-brow'd night,
Give me my Romeo; and when I shall die
Take him and cut him out in little stars,
And he will make the face of heaven so fine
That all the world will be in love with night,
And pay no worship to the garish sun.

**Context:** Romeo and Juliet have fallen in love, but their families are bitter enemies. With the help of their co-conspirators – Juliet's Nurse and Friar Laurence, a local monk – they have wed in secret. Here, Juliet waits impatiently for nightfall, when she can finally consummate her marriage with Romeo.

**Dates:** *The most excellent Tragedie of Romeo and Juliet* can be plausibly dated to 1594 or 1595. The play was first published in quarto in 1597, but this text is generally considered to be poor quality – the above quotation does not appear in this version. A 'newly corrected, augmented, and amended' second quarto was printed in 1599, which seems to have made use of Shakespeare's personal manuscripts.

**Image:** *Second Quarto, 1599.*

Whole note, full many a man doth marke,
And dares not anſwere, nay.
For indeede, who would ſet his wit to ſo fooliſh a birde?
Who would giue a bird the ly, though hee cry Cuckow,
neuer ſo?

*Tita.* I pray thee, gentle mortall, ſing againe.
Myne eare is much enamoured of thy note:
So is mine eye enthralled to thy ſhape,
And thy faire vertues force (perforce) doth mooue mee,
On the firſt viewe to ſay, to ſweare, I loue thee.

*Bott.* Mee thinks miſtreſſe, you ſhould haue little reaſon
for that. And yet, to ſay the truth, reaſon and loue keepe
little company together, now a daies. The more the pitty,
that ſome honeſt neighbours will not make them friends.
Nay I can gleeke, vpon occaſion.

*Tyta,* Thou art as wiſe, as thou art beautifull.

*Bott.* Not ſo neither: but if I had wit enough to get out
of this wood, I haue enough to ſerue mine owe turne.

*Tyta* Out of this wood, doe not deſire to goe:
Thou ſhalt remaine here, whether thou wilt or no.
I am a ſpirit, of no common rate:
The Sommer, ſtill, doth tend vpon my ſtate,
And I doe loue thee : therefore goe with mee.
Ile giue thee Fairies to attend on thee:
And they ſhall fetch thee Iewels, from the deepe,
And ſing, while thou, on preſſed flowers, doſt ſleepe:
And I will purge thy mortall groſſeneſſe ſo,
That thou ſhalt, like an avery ſpirit, goe.

# A MIDSUMMER NIGHT'S DREAM

## Act 3, Scene 1

**Titania:** I pray thee, gentle mortal, sing again:
Mine ear is much enamour'd of thy note;
So is mine eye enthralled to thy shape;
And thy fair virtue's force perforce doth move me
On the first view to say, to swear, I love thee.

**Context:** Titania, Queen of the Fairies, has been enchanted in her sleep on the orders of her husband, King Oberon, so that she will fall in love with the first creature that she sees. While she sleeps Puck, Oberon's attendant, comes across a group of Athenian workmen rehearsing their play in the woods. He mischievously transforms Bottom, changing his head to that of a donkey. Titania awakens from her 'flowery bed' and is instantly infatuated with the clueless Bottom.

**Dates:** *A Midsummer nights Dreame* was probably composed in 1595. Legend has it that the play was written for an aristocratic wedding, but there is no evidence to support this. It was frequently performed by Shakespeare's company, the Lord Chamberlain's Men, and was first published in quarto in 1600.

And Father Cardinall, I haue heard you say
That we shall see and know our friends in heauen:
If that be true, I shall see my boy againe;
For since the birth of *Caine*, the first male-childe
To him that did but yesterday suspire,
There was not such a gracious creature borne:
But now will Canker-sorrow eat my bud,
And chase the natiue beauty from his cheeke,
And he will looke as hollow as a Ghost,
As dim and meager as an Agues fitte,
And so hee'll dye: and rising so againe,
When I shall meet him in the Court of heauen
I shall not know him: therefore neuer, neuer
Must I behold my pretty *Arthur* more.

   *Pand.* You hold too heynous a respect of greefe.
   *Const.* He talkes to me, that neuer had a sonne.
   *Fra.* You are as fond of greefe, as of your childe.
   *Con.* Greefe fils the roome vp of my absent childe:
Lies in his bed, walkes vp and downe with me,
Puts on his pretty lookes, repeats his words,
Remembers me of all his gracious parts,
Stuffes out his vacant garments with his forme;
Then, haue I reason to be fond of griefe?
Fareyouwell: had you such a losse as I,
I could giue better comfort then you doe.
I will not keepe this forme vpon my head,
When there is such disorder in my witte:
O Lord, my boy, my *Arthur*, my faire sonne,
My life, my ioy, my food, my all the world:
My widow-comfort, and my sorrowes cure.   *Exit.*
   *Fra.* I feare some out-rage, and Ile follow her. *Exit.*
   *Dol.* There's nothing in this world can make me ioy,
Life is as tedious as a twice-told tale,
Vexing the dull eare of a drowsie man;
And bitter shame hath spoyl'd the sweet words taste,
That it yeelds nought but shame and bitternesse.

# KING JOHN

## Act 3, Scene 3

**Constance:** Grief fills the room up of my absent child,
Lies in his bed, walks up and down with me,
Puts on his pretty looks, repeats his words,
Remembers me of all his gracious parts,
Stuffs out his vacant garments with his form;
Then have I reason to be fond of grief?

**Context:** King Richard I has died, and his brother John has taken the crown. His reign is opposed by King Philip of France, who supports the claim of Arthur, Richard's young nephew by his deceased older brother Geoffrey. The two nations go to war, and Arthur is captured by John's forces. The boy's mother, Constance, hears of his fate and is convinced that he is dead.

**Dates:** Shakespeare probably wrote *The Life and Death of King John* between 1595 and 1596. His principal source is thought to have been the 1591 play *The Troublesome Reign of King John*, which was published anonymously but has been attributed to George Peele. *The Life and Death* was originally published in the First Folio of 1623.

**Image:** *First Folio, 1623.*

vſd to come ſo ſmug vpon the Mart : let him looke to his bond, he was wont to call me vſurer, let him looke to his bond, hee was wont to lende money for a Chriſtian curſie, let him looke to his bond.

*Salari.* Why I am ſure if he forfaite, thou wilt not take his fleſh, what's that good for?

*Shyl.* To baite fiſh with all, if it will feede nothing elſe, it will feede my reuenge; hee hath diſgrac'd me, and hindred me halfe a million, laught at my loſſes, mockt at my gaines, ſcorned my Nation, thwarted my bargaines, cooled my friends, heated mine enemies, and whats his reaſon, I am a Iewe: Hath not a Iewe eyes, hath not a Iewe hands, organs, dementions, ſences, affections, paſſions, fed with the ſame foode, hurt with the ſame weapons, ſubiect to the ſame diſeaſes, healed by the ſame meanes, warmed and cooled by the ſame Winter and Sommer as a Chriſtian is : if you pricke vs doe we not bleede, if you tickle vs doe wee not laugh, if you poyſon vs doe wee not die, and if you wrong vs ſhall wee not reuenge, if we are like you in the reſt, we will reſemble you in that. If a Iewe wrong a Chriſtian, what is his humillity, reuenge? If a Chriſtian wrong a Iewe, what ſhould his ſufferance be by Chriſtian example, why reuenge? The villanie you teach me I will execute, and it ſhall goe hard but I will better the inſtruction.

*Enter a man from* Anthonio.

Gentlemen, my maiſter *Anthonio* is at his houſe, and deſires to ſpeake with you both.

*Saleri.* We haue beene vp and downe to ſeeke him.

*Enter* Tuball.

*Solanio.* Heere comes another of the Tribe, a third cannot bee matcht, vnleſſe the deuill himſelfe turne Iewe. *Exeunt Gentlemen.*

*Enter* Tuball.

*Shy.* How now *Tuball*, what newes from Genowa, haſt thou found my daughter?

*Tuball.* I often came where I did heare of her, but cannot finde her.

# THE MERCHANT OF VENICE
## Act 3, Scene 1

**Shylock:** He hath disgrac'd me, and hind'red me half a million, laugh'd at my losses, mock'd at my gains, scorned my nation, thwarted my bargains, cooled my friends, heated mine enemies, – and what's his reason? I am a Jew. Hath not a Jew eyes? hath not a Jew hands, organs, dimensions, senses, affections, passions? fed with the same food, hurt with the same weapons, subject to the same diseases, healed by the same means, warmed and cooled by the same winter and summer as a Christian is? – if you prick us do we not bleed? if you tickle us do we not laugh? if you poison us do we not die? and if you wrong us shall we not revenge?

**Context:** Jewish Shylock has been asked to lend money to his old enemy, Antonio. He agrees, but insists upon a costly penalty if repayment is not made – a pound of Antonio's flesh. In conversation with two of Antonio's acquaintances, Shylock expresses delight at the news that his debtor looks set for bankruptcy, and speaks emotionally of the discrimination that he has faced at Antonio's hands.

**Dates:** *The comical History of the Merchant of Venice* was probably written between 1596 and 1597 and had certainly been performed by 1598. The main plot follows that of a tale found in the fourteenth-century Italian collection *Il Pecorone*, which Shakespeare may have read in translation or found elsewhere. *The Merchant of Venice* was first published in quarto in 1600.

ly,both in word and matter,hang me vp by the heeles for a rab-
bet fucker,or a poulters Hare

 *Prin.* Well,here I am fet.

 *Fal.* And here I ftand,iudge my maifters.

 *Prin.* Now Harry,whence come you?

 *Fal.* My noble Lord from Eaftcheape.

 *Prin.* The complaints I heare of thee are greeuous.

 *Fal.* Zbloud my Lord they are falfe:nay ile tickle ye for a yong
prince I faith.

 *Prin.* Sweareft thou vngratious boy, hence forth nere looke
on me,thou art violently carried awaie from grace, there is a diuell haunts thee in the likeneffe of an olde fat man , a tun of man
is thy companion : why doeft thou conuerfe with that trunke of
humours,that boultinghutch of beaftlineffe, that fwolne parcell
of dropfies that huge bombard of facke, that ftuft cloakebag of
guts, that rofted Manningtre Oxe with the pudding in his belly,
that reuerent vice,that gray iniquity,that father ruffian ,that vanity in yeares,wherein is he good,but to taft facke and drinke it?
wherein neat and clenly,but to carue a capon and eat it?wherein
cunning,but in craft?wherein crafty,but in villany?wherein villanous,but in al things?where in worthy,but in nothing?

 *Fal.* I would your grace would take me with you, whome
meanes your grace?

 *Prin.* That villanous abhominable mifleader of youth, Fal-
ftalffe,that olde white bearded Sathan.

 *Fal.* My Lord,the man I know.

 *Prin.* I know thou doeft.

 *Fal.* But to fay I knowe more harme in him then in my felfe,
were to fay more then I know : that he is olde the more the pittie, his white haires doe witneffe it,but that he is fauing your re-
uerence,a whoremafter,that I vtterlie denie : if facke and fugar
be a fault,God helpe the wicked;if to be olde and merry be a fin,

# KING HENRY IV, PART 1

## Act 2, Scene 4

**Prince Henry:** Thou art violently carried away from grace, there is a devil haunts thee in the likeness of an old fat man, a tun of man is thy companion. Why dost thou converse with that trunk of humours, that bolting-hutch of beastliness, that swollen parcel of dropsies, that huge bombard of sack, that stuffed cloak-bag of guts, that roasted Manningtree ox with the pudding in his belly, that reverend vice, that grey iniquity, that father ruffian, that vanity in years?

**Context:** Henry Bolingbroke has successfully ousted Richard II and taken the crown for himself. His reign is troubled by disloyal nobles, his own guilty conscience, and the behaviour of his wayward son, Prince Henry. The Prince is well aware of his father's disapproval of his riotous companions, particularly the rotund and dissolute Sir John Falstaff. During a drinking spree, Prince Henry pretends to be his father and in this speech admonishes Falstaff for his gluttony.

**Dates:** *King Henry IV, Part 1* was probably written and performed in 1596 or 1597. There is evidence that the character of Falstaff was originally named Sir John Oldcastle, after a famous Protestant martyr, but the playing company may have been compelled to change this to avoid offence to Oldcastle's influential descendants. The play was first published in quarto in 1598 as *The History of Henrie the Fourth*.

*Pist.* 'Tis so indeed *Nym*, thou hast hit it right.

*Fal.* Well, afore God, I must cheat, I must cony-
catch.

Which of you knowes *Foord* of this Towne?

*Pist.* I ken the wight, he is of substance good.

*Fal.* Well my honest Lads, Ile tell you what
I am about.

*Pist.* Two yards and more.

*Fal.* No gibes now *Pistoll*: indeed I am two yards
In the wast, but now I am about no wast:
Briefly, I am about thrift you rogues you,
I do intend to make loue to *Foords* wife,
I espie entertainment in her. She carues, she
Discourses. She giues the lyre of inuitation,
And euery part to be constured rightly is, I am
Syr *Iohn Falstaffes*.

*Pist.* He hath studied her well, out of honestie
Into English.

*Fal.* Now the report goes, she hath all the rule
Of her husbands purse. She hath legians of angels.

*Pist.* As many diuels attend her.
And to her boy say I.

*Fal.* Heere's a Letter to her. Heeres another to
misteris *Page*.

# THE MERRY WIVES OF WINDSOR

## Act 1, Scene 3

**Sir John Falstaff:** No quips now, Pistol: – Indeed I am in the waist two yards about, but I am now about no waste: I am about thrift. Briefly, I do mean to make love to Ford's wife. I spy entertainment in her: she discourses, she carves, she gives the leer of invitation. I can construe the action of her familiar style, and the hardest voice of her behaviour – to be Englished rightly – is: 'I am Sir John Falstaff's'.

**Context:** Sir John Falstaff is indulging in riotous behaviour in Windsor, to the dismay of the local authorities. Convinced he has caught the eye of Mistress Ford and Mistress Page and in need of cash, he decides he can repair his fortunes (and satisfy his lechery) by seducing the respectable Mistress Ford.

**Dates:** *The Merry Wives of Windsor* was written in response to the enormous popularity of the character of Falstaff from *Henry IV*; legend has it that Queen Elizabeth I herself requested a new love adventure for the portly knight. Records suggest the play may have been written in 1597 and performed later that year at the Garter Feast at Whitehall on St George's Day. It was first published in a 'bad' quarto in 1602, so called because the text was much shorter and contained significant differences to that of the First Folio of 1623.

**Image:** *First Quarto, 1602.*

*Falst.* God faue thy grace King Hall, my royall Hall.

*Pist.* The heauens thee gard and keep, moſt royal impe of fame.

*Falst.* God faue thee, my ſweet boy.

*King* My Lord chiefe iuſtice, ſpeake to that vaine man.

*Iust.* Haue you your wits? know you what tis you ſpeake?

*Falst.* My King, my Ioue, I ſpeake to thee, my heart.

*King* I know thee not old man, fall to thy praiers,
How ill white heires becomes a foole and ieſter,
I haue long dreampt of ſuch a kind of man,
So ſurfet-ſweld, ſo old, and ſo prophane:
But being awakt, I do deſpiſe my dreame,
Make leſſe thy body (hence) and more thy grace,
Leaue gourmandizing, know the graue doth gape
For thee, thrice wider then for other men,
Reply not to me with a foole-borne ieſt,
Preſume not that I am the thing I was,
For God doth know, ſo ſhall the world perceiue,
That I haue turnd away my former ſelfe,
So will I thoſe that kept me company:
When thou doſt heare I am as I haue bin,
Approch me, and thou ſhalt be as thou waſt,
The tutor and the feeder of my riots:
Till then I baniſh thee, on paine of death,
As I haue done the reſt of my miſleaders,
Not to come neare our perſon by ten mile:
For competence of life, I wil allow you,
That lacke of meanes enforce you not to euills,
And as we heare you do reforme your ſelues,
We will according to your ſtrengths and qualities,
Giue you aduauncement. Be it your charge my lord

# KING HENRY IV, PART 2

## Act 5, Scene 5

**Prince Henry:** I know thee not, old man. Fall to thy prayers.
How ill white hairs becomes a fool and jester!
I have long dreamt of such a kind of man,
So surfeit-swell'd, so old, and so profane;
But being awak'd I do despise my dream.
Make less thy body hence, and more thy grace;
Leave gormandizing; know the grave doth gape
For thee thrice wider than for other men.
Reply not to me with a fool-born jest;
Presume not that I am the thing I was;

**Context:** King Henry IV continues to struggle against the Earl of
Northumberland and his rebellion. On his deathbed he is reconciled with
Prince Henry, who realises he must change his ways to hold his father's
throne. In the final scene, the newly crowned King Henry V renounces
his old friend Falstaff.

**Dates:** *King Henry IV, Part 2* was probably written between 1597 and
1598. It is unclear whether Shakespeare originally planned to write a two-
part piece. *Part 2* seems to act more as a sequel to *Henry IV, Part 1* than as
the second half of a complete story. It was first published in quarto in 1600
as *The Second part of Henrie the fourth.*

**Image:** *First Quarto, 1600.*

Speaking my fancy: Signior Benedicke,
For shape, for bearing argument and valour,
Goes formost in report through Italy.

*Hero* Indeed he hath an excellent good name.

*Vrsula* His excellence did earne it, ere he had it:
When are you married madame?

*Hero* Why euery day to morrow, come go in,
Ile shew thee some attyres, and haue thy counsaile,
Which is the best to furnish me to morrow.

*Vrsula* Shees limed I warrant you,
We haue caught her madame.

*Hero* If it proue so, then louing goes by haps,
Some Cupid kills with arrowes some with traps.

*Beat.* What fire is in mine eares? can this be true?
Stand I condemn'd for pride and scorne so much?
Contempt, farewel, and maiden pride, adew,
No glory liues behind the backe of such.
And Benedicke, loue on I will requite thee,
Taming my wild heart to thy louing hand:
If thou dost loue, my kindnesse shall incite thee
To bind our loues vp in a holy band.
For others say thou dost deserue, and I

E

Beleeue it better then reportingly.                    *exit.*

*Enter Prince, Claudio, Benedicke, and Leonato.*

*Prince* I doe but stay til your mariage be consummate, and
then go I toward Arragon.

# MUCH ADO ABOUT NOTHING

## Act 3, Scene 1

**Beatrice:** What fire is in mine ears? Can this be true?
    Stand I condemn'd for pride and scorn so much?
Contempt, farewell, and maiden pride, adieu!
    No glory lives behind the back of such.
And, Benedick, love on, I will requite thee,
    Taming my wild heart to thy loving hand.
If thou dost love, my kindness shall incite thee
    To bind our loves up in a holy band;
    For others say thou dost deserve, and I
    Believe it better than reportingly.

**Context:** Don Pedro, Prince of Aragon, is visiting Leonato, Governor of Messina. Accompanying Pedro are his followers Benedick and Claudio, the former of whom is a sworn enemy to love. Benedick clashes with Beatrice, Leonato's spirited niece, but their friends suspect that the two may make a perfect match. First Benedick and then Beatrice are tricked into eavesdropping on conversations in which one's love for the other is revealed, causing each to recognise their true feelings for one another.

**Dates:** *Much Ado About Nothing* was probably written between spring 1598 and summer 1599. It appears that Shakespeare wrote the part of Dogberry, a constable, for comic actor Will Kemp. The play was first published in quarto in 1600.

*Bedford* and *Exeter*, *Clarence* and *Gloster*,
*Warwick* and *Yorke*.
Familiar in their mouthes as houfhold words.
This ftory fhall the good man tell his fonne,
And from this day, vnto the generall doome:
But we in it fhall be remembred.

We fewe, we happie fewe, we bond of brothers,
For he to day that fheads his blood by mine,
Shalbe my brother: be he nere fo bafe,
This day fhall gentle his condition.
Then fhall he ftrip his fleeues, and fhew his skars,
And fay, thefe wounds I had on Crifpines day:
And Gentlemen in England now a bed,
Shall thinke themfelues accurft,
And hold their manhood cheape,
While any fpeake that fought with vs
Vpon Saint Crifpines day.

*Gloft.* My gracious Lord,
The French is in the field.
*Kin.* Why all things are ready, if our minds be fo.
*War.* Perifh the man whofe mind is backward now.
*King.* Thou doft not wifh more help frõ England coufe
*War.* Gods will my Liege, would you and I alone,
Without more helpe, might fight this battle out.

*King.* W

# KING HENRY V

## Act 4, Scene 3

**King Henry:** We few, we happy few, we band of brothers.
For he today that sheds his blood with me
Shall be my brother; be he ne'er so vile,
This day shall gentle his condition.
And gentlemen in England now abed
Shall think themselves accursed they were not here,
And hold their manhoods cheap whiles any speaks
That fought with us upon Saint Crispin's day.

**Context:** England is at war with France, and the English Army is
on campaign. The soldiers, outnumbered five to one, are thoroughly
demoralised. Before the Battle of Agincourt, King Henry fires the valour of
his soldiers with this rousing, patriotic speech.

**Dates:** *The Chronicle History of Henry the fift* was first published in quarto
in 1600. Topical references in the play suggest that it was probably written
and performed in 1599. The quarto edition is half as long as that of the
First Folio, largely due to the omission of the Chorus: in the later text, they
set the scene and introduce each act.

ir Reasons,

ce.

are mee for my
Beleeue me for
nor, that you
om, and awake
e. If there bee
Cæfars, to him
ffe then his. If
fe againft Cæ-
far leffe, but
Cæfar were li-
were dead, to
veepe for him;
was Valiant, I
lew him. There
ne : Honor, for

Who is heere
,fpeak, for him
that would not
offended. Who
ntrey ? If any,
or a Reply.

I haue done no
s. The Quefti-
his Glory not
his offences en-

rs body.

ke Antony, who
receiue the be-

---

3 He fayes, for Brutus fake

He findes himfelfe beholding to vs all.

 4 'Twere beft he fpeake no harme of *Brutus* heere ?

 1 This *Cæsar* was a Tyrant.

 3 Nay that's certaine :

We are bleft that Rome is rid of him.

 2 Peace, let vs heare what *Antony* can fay.

*Ant.* You gentle Romans.

*All.* Peace hoe, let vs heare him.

*An.* Friends, Romans, Countrymen, lend me your ears:
I come to bury *Cæsar*, not to praife him :
The euill that men do, liues after them,
The good is oft enterred with their bones,
So let it be with *Cæsar*. The Noble *Brutus*,
Hath told you *Cæsar* was Ambitious :
If it were fo, it was a greeuous Fault,
And greeuoufly hath *Cæsar* anfwer'd it.
Heere, vnder leaue of *Brutus*, and the reft
(For *Brutus* is an Honourable man,
So are they all; all Honourable men)
Come I to fpeake in *Cæsars* Funerall.
He was my Friend, faithfull, and iuft to me ;
But *Brutus* fayes, he was Ambitious,
And *Brutus* is an Honourable man.

He hath brought many Captiues home to Rome,
Whofe Ranfomes, did the generall Coffers fill :
Did this in *Cæsar* feeme Ambitious ?
When that the poore haue cry'de, *Cæsar* hath wept :
Ambition fhould be made of fterner ftuffe,
Yet *Brutus* fayes, he was Ambitious :
And *Brutus* is an Honourable man.
You all did fee, that on the *Lupercall*,
I thrice prefented him a Kingly Crowne,
Which he did thrice refufe. Was this Ambition ?
Yet *Brutus* fayes, he was Ambitious :
And fure he is an Honourable man.
I fpeake not to difprooue what *Brutus* fpoke,
But heere I am, to fpeake what I do know ;

# JULIUS CAESAR

## Act 3, Scene 2

**Mark Anthony:** Friends, Romans, countrymen, lend me your ears:
I come to bury Caesar, not to praise him.
The evil that men do lives after them:
The good is oft interred with their bones.
So let it be with Caesar. The noble Brutus
Hath told you Caesar was ambitious:
If it were so, it was a grievous fault,
And grievously hath Caesar answered it.
Here, under leave of Brutus and the rest
(For Brutus is an honourable man;
So are they all, all honourable men)
Come I to speak in Caesar's funeral.
He was my friend, faithful and just to me;
But Brutus says, he was ambitious,
And Brutus is an honourable man.

**Context:** Julius Caesar has grown too ambitious and his senators fear he
will turn tyrant. Brutus, Cassius, and their fellow conspirators lure him
to the senate house and stab him to death on the Ides of March. At first,
Brutus is able to convince the crowd at Caesar's funeral that the murder was
justified, but Mark Anthony's skilful speech soon turns the mood against
the conspirators.

**Dates:** *The Tragedy of Julius Caesar* was possibly written to open the new
Globe Theatre in London in 1599. It was the first of Shakespeare's plays
to draw on an English translation of Plutarch's *Lives of the Noble Grecians
and Romans*. The play was originally published in the First Folio of 1623.

**Image:** *First Folio, 1623.*

Ros. Now tell me how long you would haue her, after you haue possest her?

Orl. For euer, and a day.

Ros. Say a day, without the euer: no, no Orlando, men
are Aprill when they woe, December when they wed:
Maides are May when they are maides, but the sky changes when they are wiues: I will bee more iealous of
thee, then a Barbary cocke-pidgeon ouer his hen, more
clamorous then a Parrat against raine, more new-fang-
led then an ape, more giddy in my desires, then a mon-
key: I will weepe for nothing, like Diana in the Foun-
taine, & I wil do that when you are dispos'd to be merry:
I will laugh like a Hyen, and that when thou art inclin'd
to sleepe.

Orl. But will my Rosalind doe so?

Ros. By my life, she will doe as I doe.

Orl. O but she is wise.

Ros. Or else shee could not haue the wit to doe this:
the wiser, the waywarder: make the doores vpon a womans wit, and it will out at the casement: shut that, and
'twill out at the key-hole: stop that, 'twill flie with the
smoake out at the chimney.

Orl. A man that had a wife with such a wit, he might
say, wit whether wil't?

Ros. Nay, you might keepe that checke for it, till you
met your wiues wit going to your neighbours bed.

Orl. And what wit could wit haue, to excuse that?

Rosa. Marry to say, she came to seeke you there: you
shall neuer take her without her answer, vnlesse you take
her without her tongue: ô that woman that cannot
make her fault her husbands occasion, let her neuer nurse
her childe her selfe, for she will breed it like a foole.

Orl. For these two houres Rosalinde, I wil leaue thee.

Ros. Alas, deere loue, I cannot lacke thee two houres.

Orl. I must attend the Duke at dinner, by two a clock
I will be with thee againe.

# AS YOU LIKE IT

## Act 4, Scene 1

**Rosalind:** Say a day, without the ever. No, no, Orlando, men are April when they woo, December when they wed. Maids are May when they are maids, but the sky changes when they are wives.

**Context:** Orlando and Rosalind have fallen in love at first sight. She is forced to flee from court to the Forest of Arden; Orlando, too, flees to the forest from his murderous brother Oliver. When their paths cross Orlando does not recognise Rosalind, who has disguised herself as a boy for safety, and taken the name Ganymede. She offers to tutor him in love so that he may win the heart of Rosalind, and here warns him of the transience of love.

**Dates:** *As You Like It* was probably written and first performed between 1599 and 1600. Shakespeare used the plot of Thomas Lodge's prose romance *Rosalynde: Euphues' Golden Legacy* (1590). The play was originally published in the First Folio of 1623.

**Image:** *First Folio, 1623.*

" Graple them to thee with a hoope of steele,
" But do not dull the palme with entertaine,
" Of euery new vnfleg'd courage,
" Beware of entrance into a quarrell; but being in,
" Beare it that the opposed may beware of thee,
" Costly thy apparrell, as thy purse can buy.
" But not exprest in fashion,
" For the apparell oft proclaimes the man.
And they of *France* of the chiefe rancke and station
Are of a most select and generall chiefe in that:
" This aboue all, to thy owne selfe be true,
And it must follow as the night the day,

Thou

Thou canst not then be false to any one,
Farewel, my blessing with thee.
   *Lear.* I humbly take my leaue, farewell *Ofelia*,
And remember well what I haue said to you.   *exit.*
   *Ofel.* It is already lock't within my hart,
And you your selfe shall keepe the key of it.
   *Cor.* What i'st *Ofelia* he hath saide to you?
   *Ofel.* Somthing touching the prince *Hamlet.*
   *Cor.* Mary wel thought on, t'is giuen me to vnderstand
That you haue bin too prodigall of your maiden presence
Vnto Prince Hamlet, if it be so,
As so tis giuen to mee, and that in waie of caution
I must tell you; you do not vnderstand your selfe
So well as befits my honor, and your credite.

# HAMLET

## Act 1, Scene 3

**Polonius:** This above all: to thine own self be true,
And it must follow as the night the day
Thou canst not then be false to any man.

**Context:** The King of Denmark is dead, and his brother Claudius has inherited the throne – and married his widow. Polonius is councillor of state to King Claudius, and father to Laertes and Ophelia. After Laertes warns his sister to stay away from the troubled Prince Hamlet, Polonius lectures his son on appropriate conduct during his impending travels in France.

**Dates:** *The Tragicall Historie of Hamlet, Prince of Denmarke* has been dated to 1600 and has a complex history in print. The play was first published in a 'bad' quarto edition in 1603; the 'good' quarto of 1604–05 has a text that is nearly twice as long and often quite different; the version that appears in the First Folio of 1623 is different yet again. It is generally agreed that the 'good' quarto was printed from Shakespeare's original manuscript, while the Folio text is the revised theatrical edition. The provenance of the 1603 quarto is still contested. In this edition, Polonius is named 'Corambis'.

is excellent at faults.

*Mal.* *M.* But then there is no confonancy in the fequell that fuffers vnder probation : *A.* fhould follow, but *O.* does.

*Fa.* And *O* fhall end, I hope.

*To.* I, or Ile cudgell him, and make him cry *O.*

*Mal.* And then *I.* comes behind.

*Fa.* I, and you had any eye behinde you, you might fee more detraction at your heeles, then Fortunes before you.

*Mal.* *M,O,A,I.* This fimulation is not as the former: and yet to crufh this a little, it would bow to mee, for e-uery one of thefe Letters are in my name. Soft, here fol-lowes profe : *If this fall into thy hand, reuolue.* In my ftars I am aboue thee, but be not affraid of greatneffe : Some are become great, fome atcheeues greatneffe, and, fome haue greatneffe thruft vppon em. Thy fates open theyr hands, let thy blood and fpirit embrace them, and to in-vre thy felfe to what thou art like to be : caft thy humble flough, and appeare frefh. Be oppofite with a kinfman, furly with feruants : Let thy tongue tang arguments of ftate ; put thy felfe into the tricke of fingularitie. Shee thus aduifes thee, that fighes for thee. Remember who commended thy yellow ftockings, and wifh'd to fee thee euer croffe garter'd : I fay remember, goe too, thou art made if thou defir'ft to be fo : If not, let me fee thee a fte-ward ftill, the fellow of feruants, and not woorthie to touch Fortunes fingers Farewell, Shee that would alter feruices with thee, tht fortunate vnhappy daylight and champian difcouers not more : This is open, I will bee proud, I will reade politicke Authours, I will baffle Sir *Toby,* I will wafh off groffe acquaintance, I will be point deuife, the very man. I do not now foole my felfe, to let imagination iade mee ; for euery reafon excites to this, that my Lady loues me. She did commend my yellow ftockings of late, fhee did praife my legge being croffe-garter'd, and in this fhe manifefts her felfe to my loue, & with a kinde of iniunction driues mee to thefe habites of her liking. I thanke my ftarres, I am happy : I will bee ftrange, ftout, in yellow ftockings, and croffe Garter'd,

his firft approach before my Lady : in yellow ftockings, and 'tis a col— croffe garter'd, a fafhion fhee dete— vpon her, which will now be fo vn— fition, being addicted to a melanch— cannot but turn him into a notable fee it follow me.

*To.* To the gates of Tartar, thou of wit.

*And.* Ile make one too.

---

## *Actus Tertius, Sc*

*Enter Viola and Clo*

*Vio.* Saue thee Friend and thy by thy Tabor?

*Clo.* No fir, I liue by the Churc

*Vio.* Art thou a Churchman?

*Clo.* No fuch matter fir, I do li I do liue at my houfe, and my hou Church.

*Vio.* So thou maift fay the King begger dwell neer him : or the Ch bor, if thy Tabor ftand by the Ch

*Clo.* You haue faid fir : To fee t but a cheu'rill gloue to a good w wrong fide may be turn'd outwar

*Vio.* Nay that's certaine : they words, may quickely make them v

*Clo.* I would therefore my fifte

*Vio.* Why man ?

*Clo.* Why fir, her names a w that word, might make my fifter words are very Rafcals, fince bon—

*Vio.* Thy reafon man ?

# TWELFTH NIGHT

## Act 2, Scene 5

**Malvolio:** Some are born great, some achieve greatness, and some have greatness thrust upon 'em. Thy fates open their hands, let thy blood and spirit embrace them, and to inure thyself to what thou art like to be, cast thy humble slough, and appear fresh.

**Context:** Countess Olivia is being courted by Orsino, the Duke of Illyria. She is falling instead for his messenger, a shipwrecked girl named Viola who has disguised herself as a boy. In Olivia's household her kinsman Sir Toby Belch, his drinking partner Sir Andrew Aguecheek, and the servant Maria play a cruel trick on the pompous steward Malvolio. They plant a false letter for him to discover, in which 'Olivia' proclaims her love for Malvolio and provides reassurance that the difference in their ranks can be overcome.

**Dates:** *Twelfth Night, or What You Will* was probably written and performed in 1601. The first recorded performance was held at the Middle Temple law school in London on Candlemas (2 February) 1602. The play was originally published in the First Folio of 1623.

**Image:** *First Folio, 1623.*

Yet hold I off : women are angels woing,
,,Things woone are done, ioyes foule lies in the dooing.
That ſhee belou'd, knows naught that knows not this,
,,Men price the thing vngaind more then it is,
That ſhe was neuer yet that euer knew
Loue got ſo ſweet, as when deſire did ſue,
Therefore this *maxim* out of loue I teach,
" *Atchiuement is command; vngaind beſeech,*
Then though my hearts content firme loue doth beare,
Nothing of that ſhall from mine eyes appeare.     *Exit.*

*Enter* Agamemnon, Neſtor, Vliſſes, Diomedes,
Menelaus *with others.*

*Aga.* Princes: what griefe hath ſet theſe Iaundies ore your
The ample propoſition that hope makes,          (cheekes?
In all deſignes begun on earth below,
Failes in the promiſt largeneſſe, checks and diſaſters,
Grow in the vaines of actions higheſt reard,
As knots by the conflux of meeting ſap,
Infects the ſound Pine, and diuerts his graine;
Tortiue and errant from his courſe of growth,
Nor Princes is it matter new to vs,
That we come ſhort of our ſuppoſe ſo farre,
That after ſeauen yeares ſiege, yet Troy walls ſtand;
Sith euer action that hath gone before,
Whereof we haue record, triall did draw,
Bias and thwart : not anſwering the ayme,
And that vnbodied figure of the thought,
That gau't ſurmiſed ſhape: why then you Princes,
Do you with cheekes abaſht behold our workes,

# TROILUS AND CRESSIDA

## Act 1, Scene 2

**Cressida:**        Women are angels, wooing;
Things won are done; joy's soul lies in the doing.
That she beloved knows naught that knows not this:
Men prize the thing ungained more than it is.
That she was never yet that ever knew
Love got so sweet as when desire did sue.
Therefore this maxim out of love I teach:
'Achievement is command; ungained, beseech'.
Then, though my heart's contents firm love doth bear,
Nothing of that shall from mine eyes appear.

**Context:** The Greeks have been besieging Troy for seven years, and the war has reached a stalemate. Cressida, whose father has defected to the Greeks, is being wooed by Prince Troilus. She feigns disinterest, concealing her true feelings from both Troilus and her interfering uncle Pandarus. Here, Cressida reveals the motivation behind her pretence.

**Dates:** *Troilus and Cressida* was probably written between 1601 and 1603. Shakespeare drew on several sources: the story of the siege of Troy first appeared in Homer's *Iliad*, but Geoffrey Chaucer's fourteenth-century poem *Troilus and Criseyde* appears to have been particularly influential. The play was first published in quarto in 1609.

**Image:** *First Quarto, 1609.*

But for their virtue only is their ſhow,
They liue vnwoo'd, and vnreſpected fade,
Die to themſelues . Sweet Roſes doe not ſo,
Of their ſweet deathes, are ſweeteſt odors made:
  And ſo of you, beautious and louely youth,
  When that ſhall vade, by verſe diſtils your truth.

## 55

NOt marble, nor the guilded monument,
  Of Princes ſhall out-liue this powrefull rime,
But you ſhall ſhine more bright in theſe contents
Then vnſwept ſtone, beſmeer'd with ſluttiſh time.
When waſtefull warre ſhall *Statues* ouer-turne,
And broiles roote out the worke of maſonry,
Nor *Mars* his ſword, nor warres quick fire ſhall burne
The liuing record of your memory.

Gainſt

Gainſt death, and all obliuious emnity
Shall you pace forth, your praiſe ſhall ſtil finde roome,
Euen in the eyes of all poſterity
That weare this world out to the ending doome.
  So til the iudgement that your ſelfe ariſe,
  You liue in this, and dwell in louers eies.

## 56

Sweet loue renew thy force, be it not ſaid
  Thy edge ſhould blunter be then apetite,
Which but too daie by feeding is alaied,
To morrow ſharpned in his former might.
So loue be thou, although too daie thou fill
Thy hungrie eies, euen till they winck with fulneſſe,

# SONNET 55

Not marble, nor the gilded monuments
Of princes, shall outlive this powerful rhyme;
But you shall shine more bright in these contents
Than unswept stone, besmeared with sluttish time.
When wasteful war shall statues overturn
And broils root out the work of masonry,
Nor Mars his sword, nor war's quick fire, shall burn
The living record of your memory:
'Gainst death, and all oblivious enmity,
Shall you pace forth; your praise shall still find room
Even in the eyes of all posterity
That wear this world out to the ending doom.
  So till the judgement that yourself arise,
  You live in this, and dwell in lovers' eyes.

**Context:** Sonnet 55 is part of a sequence of sonnets addressed to a beautiful young man of high status. Many of these trace the ebb and flow of the relationship between the subject and the speaker. This sonnet is a testament to the power of verse against the ravages of time, and states that the author's words will prove an enduring commemoration of his beloved subject.

**Dates:** The volume entitled *Shake-speares Sonnets* was first published in 1609, but the individual poems are believed to have been written over a longer period, spanning almost two decades. It has long been speculated that the sonnets are Shakespeare's most autobiographical works, and that such apparently personal material was never intended to reach a public audience; others argue that the careful ordering of the poems in the first quarto indicates that Shakespeare not only authorised but oversaw the printing process.

**Image:** *First Quarto, 1609.*

## 120

MY Miſtres eyes are nothing like the Sunne,
Currall is farre more red,then her lips red,
If ſnow be white,why then her breſts are dun:
If haires be wiers,black wiers grow on her head:
I haue ſeene Roſes damaskt,red and white,
But no ſuch Roſes ſee I in her cheekes,
And in ſome perfumes is there more delight,
Then in the breath that from my Miſtres reekes.
I loue to heare her ſpeake,yet well I know,
That Muſicke hath a farre  more pleaſing ſound:
I graunt I neuer ſaw a goddeſſe goe,
My Miſtres when ſhee walkes treads on the ground,
    And yet by heauen I thinke my loue as rare,
    As any ſhe beli'd with falſe compare.

## 131

THou art as tiranous,ſo as thou art,
As thoſe whoſe beauties proudly make them cruell
For well thou know'ſt to my deare doting hart
Thou art the faireſt and moſt precious Iewell.
Yet in good faith ſome ſay that thee behold,
Thy face hath not the power to make loue grone;
To ſay they erre,I dare not be ſo bold,
Although I ſweare it to my ſelfe alone.

# SONNET 130

My mistress' eyes are nothing like the sun;
Coral is far more red than her lips' red;
If snow be white, why then her breasts are dun;
If hairs be wires, black wires grow on her head;
I have seen roses damasked, red and white,
But no such roses see I in her cheeks;
And in some perfumes is there more delight
Than in the breath that from my mistress reeks.
I love to hear her speak, yet well I know
That music hath a far more pleasing sound;
I grant I never saw a goddess go;
My mistress when she walks treads on the ground.
     And yet, by heaven, I think my love as rare
     As any she belied with false compare.


**Context:** Sonnet 130 is part of a sequence of sonnets addressed to the speaker's mistress, sometimes referred to as his 'Dark Lady'. In 130, Shakespeare satirizes poetic conventions of the day by comparing his lover unfavourably to the beauty of nature. The last two lines, however, reflect on the powerful love he feels for his mistress in spite of these human flaws.

**Dates:** The volume entitled *Shake-speares Sonnets* was first published in 1609, but the individual poems are believed to have been written over a longer period, spanning almost two decades. It has long been speculated that the sonnets are Shakespeare's most autobiographical works, and that such apparently personal material was never intended to reach a public audience; others argue that the careful ordering of the poems in the first quarto indicates that Shakespeare not only authorised but oversaw the printing process.

**Image:** *First Quarto, 1609.*

I gesse one angel in an others hel,
Yet this shal I nere know but liue in doubt,
Till my bad angel fire my good one out.

145

THose lips that Loues owne hand did make,
Breath'd forth the sound that said I hate,
To me that languisht for her sake:
But when she saw my wofull state,
Straight in her heart did mercie come,
Chiding that tongue that euer sweet,
Was vsde in giuing gentle dome:
And tought it thus a new to greete:
I hate she alterd with an end,
That follow'd it as gentle day,
Doth follow night who like a fiend
From heauen to hell is flowne away.
I hate, from hate away she threw,
And sau'd my life saying not you.

146

POore soule the center of my sinfull earth,
My sinfull earth these rebbell powres that thee array,
Why dost thou pine within and suffer dearth
Painting thy outward walls so costlie gay?
Why so large cost hauing so short a lease,
Dost thou vpon thy fading mansion spend?
Shall wormes inheritors of this excesse,
Eate vp thy charge? is this thy bodies end?

# SONNET 145

Those lips that love's own hand did make
Breathed forth the sound that said 'I hate',
To me, that languished for her sake;
But when she saw my woeful state,
Straight in her heart did mercy come,
Chiding that tongue that, ever sweet,
Was used in giving gentle doom,
And taught it thus anew to greet:
'I hate' she altered with an end
That followed it as gentle day
Doth follow night, who like a fiend
From heaven to hell is flown away.
    'I hate' from 'hate' away she threw,
    And saved my life, saying, 'not you'.

**Context:** Sonnet 145 may have been the first that Shakespeare ever penned. It recounts the speaker's despair when he fears he is the subject of his mistress's hatred, and his relief when she takes pity and reassures him. Because of the wordplay in the last two lines, some believe that it was written for Shakespeare's wife, Anne Hathaway.

**Dates:** The volume entitled *Shake-speares Sonnets* was first published in 1609, but the individual poems are believed to have been written over a longer period, spanning almost two decades. It has long been speculated that the sonnets are Shakespeare's most autobiographical works, and that such apparently personal material was never intended to reach a public audience; others argue that the careful ordering of the poems in the first quarto indicates that Shakespeare not only authorised but oversaw the printing process.

And doe him right, that anſwering one foule wrong
Liues not to act another. Be ſatisfied;
Your Brother dies to morrow; be content.

   *Iſab.* So you muſt be y firſt that giues this ſentence,
And hee, that ſuffers: Oh, it is excellent
To haue a Giants ſtrength: but it is tyrannous
To vſe it like a Giant.

   *Luc.* That's well ſaid.

   *Iſab.* Could great men thunder
As *Ioue* himſelfe do's, *Ioue* would neuer be quiet,
For euery pelting, petty Officer
Would vſe his heauen for thunder;
Nothing but thunder: Mercifull heauen,
Thou rather with thy ſharpe and ſulpherous bolt
Splits the vn-wedgable and gnarled Oke:
Then the ſoft Mertill: But man, proud man,
Dreſt in a little briefe authoritie,
Moſt ignorant of what he's moſt aſſur'd,
(His glaſſie Eſſence) like an angry Ape,
Plaies ſuch phantaſtique tricks before high heauen,
As makes the Angels weepe: who with our ſpleenes,
Would all themſelues laugh mortall.

   *Luc.* Oh, to him, to him wench: he will relent,
Hee's comming: I perceiue't.

   *Pro.* Pray heauen ſhe win him.

   *Iſab.* We cannot weigh our brother with our ſelfe,
Great men may ieſt with Saints: tis wit in them,
But in the leſſe fowle prophanation.

   *Luc.* Thou'rt i'th right (Girle) more o'that.

   *Iſab.* That in the Captaine's but a chollericke word,
Which in the Souldier is flat blaſphemie.

   *Luc.* Art auis'd o'that? more on't.

   *Ang.* Why doe you put theſe ſayings vpon me?

   *Iſab.* Becauſe Authoritie, though it erre like others,
Hath yet a kinde of medicine in it ſelfe
That skins the vice o'th top; goe to your boſome,
Knock there, and aske your heart what it doth know
That's like my brothers fault: if it confeſſe
A naturall guiltineſſe, ſuch as is his,
Let it not ſound a thought vpon your tongue
Againſt my brothers life.

   *Ang.* Shee ſpeakes, and 'tis ſuch ſence
That my Sence breeds with it: fare you well.

   *Ang.* From thee: euen from
What's this? what's this? is this
The Tempter, or the Tempted, w
Not ſhe: nor doth ſhe tempt: bu
That, lying by the Violet in the S
Doe as the Carrion do's, not as t
Corrupt with vertuous ſeaſon:
That Modeſty may more betray
Then womans lightneſſe? hauing
Shall we deſire to raze the Sancti
And pitch our euils there? oh fie
What doſt thou? or what art tho
Doſt thou deſire her fowly, for th
That make her good? oh, let her
Theeues for their robbery haue a
When Iudges ſteale themſelues:
That I deſire to heare her ſpeake
And feaſt vpon her eyes? what i
Oh cunning enemy, that to catch
With Saints doſt bait thy hooke
Is that temptation, that doth go
To ſinne, in louing vertue: neuer
With all her double vigor, Art,
Once ſtir my temper: but this ve
Subdues me quite: Euer till no
When men were fond, I ſmild, an

## Scena Te

   *Enter Duke and P*

   *Duke.* Haile to you, *Pronoſt, ſo*

   *Pro.* I am the Prouoſt: whats

   *Duke.* Bound by my charity, a
I come to viſite the afflicted ſpiri
Here in the priſon; doe me the co
To let me ſee them: and to make
The nature of their crimes, that I
To them accordingly.

   *Pro.* I would do more then tha

   *Enter Iuliet.*

# MEASURE FOR MEASURE

## Act 2, Scene 2

**Isabella:**　　　But man, proud man,
Dress'd in a little brief authority,
Most ignorant of what he's most assur'd –
His glassy essence – like an angry ape
Plays such fantastic tricks before high heaven
As makes the angels weep;

**Context:** In the absence of Duke Vincentio, puritanical Angelo rules
Vienna and has decided to enforce the long-neglected laws against sexual
license. Claudio and his betrothed, Juliet, have slept together before the
church can officiate their marriage, and she is pregnant. Under the new
regime, Claudio is condemned to death. He begs his sister Isabella, a
novice, to leave the nunnery and plead for mercy on his behalf. This
she does, invoking Christian forgiveness.

**Dates:** *Measure for Measure* was probably written between 1603 and 1604,
and was performed at the court of King James I on Boxing Day 1604. It
was originally published in the First Folio of 1623, but the text appears
to have undergone some revisions. These may have been carried out by
Shakespeare or his known collaborator, Thomas Middleton.

Shapes faults that are not, I intreate you then,
From one that so imperfectly coniects,
You'd take no notice, nor build your selfe a trouble,
Out of my scattering, and vnsure obseruance;
It were not for your quiet, nor your good,
Nor for my manhood, honesty, or wisedome,
To let you know my thoughts,

    *Oth.* Zouns.

    *Iag.* Good name in man and woman's deere my Lord;
Is the immediate Iewell of our soules :
Who steales my purse, steals trash, tis something, nothing,
Twas mine, tis his, and has bin slaue to thousands :
But he that filches from me my good name,
Robs me of that, which not inriches him,
And makes me poore indeed.

    *Oth.* By heauen I'le know thy thought.

    *Iag.* You cannot, if my heart were in your hand,
Nor shall not, whilst tis in my custody :
  O beware iealousie.
It is the greene ey'd monster, which doth mocke
That meate it feedes on. That Cuckold liues in blisse,
Who certaine of his fate, loues not his wronger :
But oh, what damned minutes tells he ore,
Who dotes, yet doubts, suspects, yet strongly loues.

    *Oth.* O misery.

    *Iag.* Poore and content is rich, and rich enough,
But riches, finelesse, is as poore as winter,
To him that euer feares he shall be poore :
Good God, the soules of all my tribe defend
From iealousie.

# OTHELLO

## Act 3, Scene 3

**Iago:**    O beware, my lord, of jealousy!
It is the green-eyed monster, which doth mock
The meat it feeds on. That cuckold lives in bliss
Who, certain of his fate, loves not his wronger,
But O, what damned minutes tells he o'er
Who dotes yet doubts, suspects yet strongly loves!

**Context:** The Moor Othello, a general in the Venetian military, has married
the noblewoman Desdemona and brought her with him to his posting
in Cyprus. Iago, his trusted ensign, is filled with malice and plots to turn
Othello's passion for his new wife into his downfall. After insinuating that
Desdemona has been unfaithful with lieutenant Cassio, Iago chillingly
warns of the dangers of jealousy.

**Dates:** *The Tragedy of Othello the Moore of Venice* was probably written
between September 1603 and summer 1604. It was first printed in quarto
in 1622; the version in the First Folio of 1623 is 160 lines longer and
appears to be an alternative theatrical version.

My loues more richer then my tongue.

*Lear.* To thee and thine hereditarie euer
Remaine this ample third of our faire kingdome,
No lesse in space, validity, and pleasure,
Then that confirm'd on *Gonorill*, but now our ioy,
Although the last, not least in our deere loue,
What can you say to win a third, more opulent
Then your sisters.

*Cord.* Nothing my Lord.                              (againe.

*Lear.* How, nothing can come of nothing, speake

*Cord.* Vnhappie that I am, I cannot heaue my heart into my
mouth, I loue your Maiestie according to my bond, nor more nor
lesse.

*Lear.* Goe to, goe to, mend your speech a little,
Least it may mar your fortunes.

*Cord.* Good my Lord,
You haue begot me, bred me, loued me,
I returne those duties backe as are right fit,
Obey you, loue you, and most honour you,
Why haue my sisters husbands if they say they loue you all,
Happely when I shall wed, that Lord whose hand
Must take my plight, shall cary halfe my loue with him,
Halfe my care and duty, sure I shall neuer
Mary like my sisters, to loue my father all.

*Lear.* But goes this with thy heart ?

*Cord.* I good my Lord.

*Lear.* So yong and so vntender,

*Cord.* So yong my Lord and true.

*Lear.* Well let it be so, thy truth then be thy dower,
For by the sacred radience of the Sunne,

The

# KING LEAR

## Act 1, Scene 1

**Cordelia:**        Good my lord,
You have begot me, bred me, loved me. I
Return those duties back as are right fit,
Obey you, love you and most honour you.
Why have my sisters husbands, if they say
They love you all? Haply when I shall wed,
That lord whose hand must take my plight shall carry
Half my love with him, half my care and duty.
Sure I shall never marry like my sisters
To love my father all.

**Context:** The ageing King Lear has decided to divide his kingdom between
his three daughters. He declares that he will portion the land according to
the love each bears for him. Greedy and self-interested, Goneril and Regan
profess their absolute adoration, but Lear's favourite daughter Cordelia
refuses to flatter him. Here, she carefully elucidates the limits of her
daughterly devotion.

**Dates:** *King Lear* was probably written in 1605 or 1606; the first recorded
performance took place at the court of King James I on 26 December 1606.
It was first published as *The History of King Lear* in 1608, in a text that has
major structural differences to that printed as *The Tragedy of King Lear* in
the First Folio of 1623. Many critics argue that the 1623 text was a revision
of Shakespeare's original piece by the author himself.

**Image:** *First Quarto, 1608.*

shall's get it?

*2* True: for he beares it not about him:
'Tis hid.

*1* Is not this hee?

*All.* Where?

*2* 'Tis his description.

*3* He? I know him.

*All.* Saue thee *Timon*.

*Tim.* Now Theeues.

*All.* Soldiers, not Theeues.

*Tim.* Both too, and womens Sonnes.

*All.* We are not Theeues, but men
That much do want.

*Tim.* Your greatest want is, you want much of meat:
Why should you want? Behold, the Earth hath Rootes:
Within this Mile breake forth a hundred Springs:
The Oakes beare Mast, the Briars Scarlet Heps,
The bounteous Huswife Nature, on each bush,
Layes her full Messe before you. Want? why Want?

*1* We cannot liue on Grasse, on Berries, Water,
As Beasts, and Birds, and Fishes.

*Ti.* Nor on the Beasts themselues, the Birds & Fishes,
You must eate men. Yet thankes I must you con,
That you are Theeues profest: that you worke not
In holier shapes: For there is boundlesse Theft
In limited Professions. Rascall Theeues
Heere's Gold. Go, sucke the subtle blood o'th'Grape,
Till the high Feauor seeth your blood to froth,
And so scape hanging. Trust not the Physitian,
His Antidotes are poyson, and he slayes
Moe then you Rob: Take wealth, and liues together,
Do Villaine do, since you protest to doo't.
Like Workemen, Ile example you with Theeuery:
The Sunnes a Theefe, and with his great attraction
Robbes the vaste Sea. The Moones an arrant Theefe,
And her pale fire, she snatches from the Sunne.
The Seas a Theefe, whose liquid Surge, resolues
The Moone into Salt teares. The Earth's a Theefe,
That feeds and breeds by a composture stolne
From gen'rall excrement: each thing's a Theefe.
The Lawes, your curbe and whip, in their rough power

When man was wisht to loue his En
Grant I may euer loue, and rather w
Those that would mischeefe me, the
Has caught me in his eye, I will pres
vnto him; and as my Lord, still serue
My deerest Master.

*Tim.* Away: what art thou?

*Stew.* Haue you forgot me, Sir?

*Tim.* Why dost aske that? I hau
Then, if thou grunt'st, th'art a man.
I haue forgot thee.

*Stew.* An honest poore seruant of

*Tim.* Then I know thee not:
I neuer had honest man about me, I
I kept were Knaues, to serue in meat

*Stew.* The Gods are witnesse,
Neu'r did poore Steward weare a tru
For his vndone Lord, then mine eye

*Tim.* What, dost thou weepe?
Come neerer, then I loue thee
Because thou art a woman, and discl
Flinty mankinde: whose eyes do neu
But thorow Lust and Laughter: pit
Strange times ÿ weepe with laughin

*Stew.* I begge of you to know me
T'accept my greefe, and whil'st this
To entertaine me as your Steward st

*Tim.* Had I a Steward
So true, so iust, and now so comforta
It almost turnes my dangerous Natu
Let me behold thy face: Surely, this
Was borne of woman.
Forgiue my generall, and exceptlesse
You perpetuall sober Gods. I do pr
One honest man: Mistake me not, b
No more I pray, and hee's a Steward
How faine would I haue hated all m
And thou redeem'st thy selfe. But al
I fell with Curses.
Me thinkes thou art more honest no
For, by oppressing and betraying me

# TIMON OF ATHENS

## Act 4, Scene 3

**Timon:** The sun's a thief, and with his great attraction
Robs the vast sea; the moon's an arrant thief,
And her pale fire she snatches from the sun;
The sea's a thief, whose liquid surge resolves
The moon into salt tears; the earth's a thief,
That feeds and breeds by a composture stol'n
From gen'ral excrement; each thing's a thief.

**Context:** The rich and powerful Timon of Athens has ignored the warnings of his steward Flavius and has been ruined by his thoughtless generosity. Deserted by his former friends, he has come to hate mankind. When he recovers his fortune by finding a cache of gold, bandits try to steal it. In this bitter speech, Timon urges them to theft and murder.

**Dates:** *The Life of Timon of Athens* is difficult to date, but it may have been written between 1605 and 1606. The play was originally published in the First Folio of 1623 and is believed to be the product of a collaboration between Shakespeare and Thomas Middleton.

To haue thee crown'd withall.          *Enter Messenger.*
What is your tidings?

   *Mess.* The King comes here to Night.

   *Lady.* Thou'rt mad to say it.
Is not thy Master with him? who, wer't so,
Would haue inform'd for preparation.

   *Mess.* So please you, it is true: our *Thane* is comming:
One of my fellowes had the speed of him;
Who almost dead for breath, had scarcely more
Then would make vp his Message.

   *Lady.* Giue him tending,
He brings great newes.          *Exit Messenger.*
The Rauen himselfe is hoarse,
That croakes the fatall entrance of *Duncan*
Vnder my Battlements. Come you Spirits,
That tend on mortall thoughts, vnsex me here,
And fill me from the Crowne to the Toe, top-full
Of direst Crueltie: make thick my blood,
Stop vp th'accesse, and passage to Remorse,
That no compunctious visitings of Nature
Shake my fell purpose, nor keepe peace betweene
Th'effect, and hit. Come to my Womans Brests,
And take my Milke for Gall, you murth'ring Ministers,
Where-euer, in your sightlesse substances,
You wait on Natures Mischiefe. Come thick Night,
And pall thee in the dunnest smoake of Hell,
That my keene Knife see not the Wound it makes,
Nor Heauen peepe through the Blanket of the darke,
To cry, hold, hold.          *Enter Macbeth.*
Great Glamys, worthy Cawdor,
Greater then both, by the all-haile hereafter,
Thy Letters haue transported me beyond
This ignorant present, and I feele now
The future in the instant.

*Banq.* T
The Temp
By his loue
Smells wo
Buttrice, no
Hath made
Where the
The ayre is

   *King.*
The Loue t
Which still
How you
And thank

   *Lady.*
In euery po
Were poor
Against the
Wherewith
For those o
Heap'd vp

   *King.* W
We courst hi
To be his Pu
And his grea
To his home
We are your

   *La.* You
Haue theirs,
To make the
Still to returr

   *King.* Giu
Conduct me
And shall co

# MACBETH

## Act 1, Scene 5

**Lady Macbeth:**            Come, you Spirits
That tend on mortal thoughts, unsex me here,
And fill me, from the crown to the toe, top-full
Of direst cruelty! make thick my blood,
Stop up th'access and passage to remorse;
That no compunctious visitings of Nature
Shake my fell purpose, nor keep peace between
Th'effect and it! Come to my woman's breasts,
And take my milk for gall, you muth'ring ministers,

**Context:** Macbeth is returning from battle when he encounters a trio of witches who prophesy that he will become Thane of Cawdor and then King of Scotland. When the first part of the prophecy comes true, Macbeth writes to his wife, who resolves to ensure that he will indeed become King. Together they plot to murder King Duncan while he stays in their castle. Here, Lady Macbeth calls on the spirits to assist her in carrying out this evil deed.

**Dates:** *The Tragedy of Macbeth* is believed to have been written in 1606. The play's setting and themes suggest that it was written for King James VI of Scotland, who took the English throne in 1603. It was originally published in the First Folio of 1623, although this text shows signs of revision, probably at the hand of Thomas Middleton.

**Image:** *First Folio, 1623.*

*Dol.* I vnderstand not, Madam.

*Cleo.* I dreampt there was an Emperor *Anthony*.
Oh such another sleepe, that I might see
But such another man.

*Dol.* If it might please ye.

*Cleo.* His face was as the Heau'ns, and therein stucke
A Sunne and Moone, which kept their course, & lighted
The little o'th'earth.

*Dol.* Most Soueraigne Creature.

*Cleo.* His legges bestrid the Ocean his rear'd arme
Crested the world : His voyce was propertied
As all the tuned Spheres, and that to Friends :
But when he meant to quaile, and shake the Orbe,
He was as ratling Thunder. For his Bounty,
There was no winter in't. An *Anthony* it was,
That grew the more by reaping : His delights
Were Dolphin-like, they shew'd his backe aboue
The Element they liu'd in : In his Liuery
Walk'd Crownes and Crownets : Realms & Islands were
As plates dropt from his pocket.

*Dol.* Cleopatra.

*Cleo.* Thinke you there was, or might be such a man
As this I dreampt of?

*Dol.* Gentle Madam, no.

*Cleo.* You Lye vp to the hearing of the Gods :
But if there be, nor euer were one such
It's past the size of dreaming : Nature wants stuffe
To vie strange formes with fancie, yet t'imagine
An *Anthony* were Natures peece, 'gainst Fancie,
Condemning shadowes quite.

*Dol.* Heare me, good Madam :
Your losse is as your selfe, great ; and you beare it
As answering to the waight, would I might neuer
Ore-take pursu'de successe : But I do feele
By the rebound of yours, a greefe that suites
My very heart at roote.

*Cleo.* I thanke you sir :

# ANTONY AND CLEOPATRA
## Act 5, Scene 2

**Cleopatra:** His legs bestrid the ocean; his reared arm
Crested the world; his voice was propertied
As all the tuned spheres, and that to friends;
But when he meant to quail and shake the orb,
He was as rattling thunder. For his bounty,
There was no winter in't; an autumn it was
That grew the more by reaping. His delights
Were dolphin-like: they showed his back above
The element they lived in. In his livery
Walked crowns and crownets; realms and islands were
As plates dropped from his pocket.

**Context:** Mark Antony's love affair with Cleopatra, Queen of Egypt, has all but destroyed his reputation at home in Rome. Mounting tensions between Octavius Caesar, Antony's co-ruler, and Sextus Pompeius, a rebellious General, lead to war. Facing imminent defeat and wrongly believing Cleopatra to have committed suicide, Antony fatally stabs himself. Here, on the verge of her own destruction, Cleopatra mourns for the man she loved.

**Dates:** It is likely that *The Tragedy of Antony and Cleopatra* was written no later than 1606. Although it was entered in the Stationer's Register in May 1608, the play was first printed in the First Folio of 1623.

**Image:** *First Folio, 1623.*

Count *Rossillion* and my brother,
woodcocke, and will keepe him
n them. (musled
ill.

ay vs all vnto our selues,

: keepe him darke and safely lockt.
*Exit*

ram, and the Maide called
*Diana.*

ne that your name was *Fontybell.*

d Lord, *Diana.*

desse,

addition : but faire soule,

ath loue no qualitie?

youth light not your minde,

but a monument

you should be such a one

r you are cold and sterne,

Id be as your mother was

else was got.

was honest,

you be.

dutie, such(my Lord)

r wife.

'that :

iue against my vowes :

her, but I loue thee

et constraint, and will for euer

of seruice.

erue vs

But when you haue our Roses,

ur thornes to pricke our selues,

h our barenesse.

I sworne.

ne many oathes that makes the truth,

le vow, that is vow'd true :

that we sweare not by,

t to witnesse : then pray you tell me,

by Ioues great attributes,

, would you beleeue my oathes,

ou ill ? This ha's no holding

Bequeathed downe from many Ancestors,
Which were the greatest obloquie i'th world,
In mee to loose. Thus your owne proper wisedome
Brings in the Champion honor on my part,
Against your vaine assault.

*Ber.* Heere, take my Ring,
My house, mine honor, yea my life be thine,
And Ile be bid by thee.

*Dia.* When midnight comes, knocke at my cham-
ber window :
Ile order take, my mother shall not heare.
Now will I charge you in the band of truth,
When you haue conquer'd my yet maiden-bed,
Remaine there but an houre, nor speake to mee :
My reasons are most strong, and you shall know them,
When backe againe this Ring shall be deliuer'd :
And on your finger in the night, Ile put
Another Ring, that what in time proceeds,
May token to the future, our past deeds.
Adieu till then, then faile not : you haue wonne
A wife of me, though there my hope be done.

*Ber.* A heauen on earth I haue won by wooing thee.

*Di.* For which, liue long to thank both heauen & me,
You may so in the end.
My mother told me iust how he would woo,
As if shee sate in's heart. She sayes, all men
Haue the like oathes : He had sworne to marrie me
When his wife's dead : therfore Ile lye with him
When I am buried. Since Frenchmen are so braide,
Marry that will, I liue and die a Maid :
Onely in this disguise, I think't no sinne,
To cosen him that would vniustly winne. *Exit*

*Enter the two French Captaines, and some two or three*
*Souldiours.*

*Cap.G.* You haue not giuen him his mothers letter.

*Cap.E.* I haue deliu'red it an houre since, there is som
thing in't that stings his nature : for on the reading it,
he chang'd almost into another man.

*Cap.G.* He has much worthy blame laid vpon him,
for shaking off so good a wife, and so sweet a Lady.

*Cap.E.* Especially, hee hath incurred the euerlasting
displeasure of the King, who had euen tun'd his bounty
to sing happinesse to him. I will tell you a thing, but
you shall let it dwell darkly with you.

# ALL'S WELL THAT ENDS WELL
## Act 4, Scene 2

**Diana:** When midnight comes, knock at my chamber window;
I'll order take my mother shall not hear.
Now will I charge you in the band of truth,
When you have conquer'd my yet maiden bed,
Remain there but an hour, nor speak to me.
My reasons are most strong and you shall know them
When back again this ring shall be deliver'd;

**Context:** Helena has cured the King of France of a deadly illness, and at the King's command won Bertram in marriage. Bertram, unwilling to accept her, has set a seemingly impossible requirement: she must take his ring from his finger and conceive a child by him before he will receive her as his wife. Diana, whom Bertram wishes to seduce, plans a bed trick with Helen; she agrees to sleep with him, knowing that Helen will secretly take her place.

**Dates:** The creation of *All's Well That Ends Well* has been plausibly dated to 1606 or 1607. Shakespeare derived the plot from an English translation of Giovanni Boccaccio's *Decameron* (1353). The play was originally published in the First Folio of 1623.

Moſt wiſe in generall, tell me if thou canſt, what this maybe is, or what is like to bee, that thus hath made mee weepe.

*Hel.* I know not, but heres the Regent ſir of *Metaline*, ſpeakes nobly of her.

*Lyſ.* She neuer would tell her parentage, Being demaunded, that ſhe would ſit ſtill and weepe.

*Per.* Oh *Hellicanus*, ſtrike me honored ſir, giue mee a gaſh, put me to preſent paine, leaſt this great ſea of ioyes ruſhing vpon me, ore-beare the ſhores of my mortalitie, and drowne me with their ſweetneſſe: Oh come hither, thou that begetſt him that did thee beget, Thou that waſt borne at ſea, buried at *Tharſus*, And found at ſea agen, O *Hellicanus*, Downe on thy knees, thanke the holie Gods as loud As thunder threatens vs, this is *Marina*. What was thy mothers name? tell me, but that for truth can neuer be confirm'd inough, Though doubts did euer ſleepe.

*Mar.* Friſt ſir, I pray what is your title?

*Per.* I am *Pericles* of *Tyre*, but tell mee now my Drownd Queenes name, as in the reſt you ſayd, Thou haſt beene God-like perfit, the heir of kingdomes, And an other like to *Pericles* thy father.

*Ma.* Is it no more to be your daughter, then to ſay, my mothers name was *Thaiſa*, *Thaiſa* was my mother, who did end the minute I began.

*Pe.* Now bleſſing on thee, riſe th'art my child. Giue me freſh garments, mine owne *Hellicanus*, ſhee is not dead at *Tharſus* as ſhee ſhould haue beene by ſauage *Cleon*, ſhe ſhall tell thee all, when thou ſhalt kneele, and iuſtifie in

# PERICLES

## Act 5, Scene 1

**Pericles:** Lest this great sea of joys rushing upon me
O'erbear the shores of my mortality,
And drown me with their sweetness. O, come hither,
Thou that beget'st him that did thee beget;
Thou that wast born at sea, buried at Tharsus,
And found at sea again.

**Context:** Pericles, Prince of Tyre, has been separated from his daughter Marina for fourteen years. When he seeks her out he is told that she is dead. In fact, she has survived attempted murder, been captured by pirates, and sold into a brothel, where she remains chaste. Unaware of her true identity, Marina's admirer Lysimachus summons her to sing to the grief-stricken Pericles. When father and daughter recognise one another, Pericles is overcome with joy.

**Dates:** *Pericles, Prince of Tyre* was probably written in 1607 or 1608, and was popular for much of the early seventeenth century. It was printed in quarto in 1609 but omitted from the First Folio of 1623, probably because Shakespeare wrote only the last three acts. George Wilkins, a playwright and pamphleteer, authored the first two. In 1608, Wilkins composed a prose narrative – *The Painful Adventures of Pericles, Prynce of Tyre* – that closely followed the plot of the play.

**Image:** *First Quarto, 1609.*

From off the Rocke Tarpeian, neuer more
To enter our Rome gates. I'th'Peoples name,
I say it shall bee so.

    *All.* It shall be so, it shall be so: let him away:
Hee's banish'd, and it shall be so.

    *Com.* Heare me my Masters, and my common friends.

    *Sicin.* He's sentenc'd: No more hearing.

    *Com.* Let me speake:
I haue bene Consull, and can shew from Rome
Her Enemies markes vpon me. I do loue
My Countries good, with a respect more tender,
More holy, and profound, then mine owne life,
My deere Wiues estimate, her wombes encrease,
And treasure of my Loynes: then if I would
Speake that.

    *Sicin.* We know your drift. Speake what?

    *Bru.* There's no more to be said, but he is banish'd
As Enemy to the people, and his Countrey.
It shall bee so.

    *All.* It shall be so, it shall be so.

    *Corio.* You common cry of Curs, whose breath I hate,
As reeke a'th'rotten Fennes: whose Loues I prize,
As the dead Carkasses of vnburied men,
That do corrupt my Ayre: I banish you,
And heere remaine with your vncertaintie.
Let euery feeble Rumor shake your hearts:
Your Enemies, with nodding of their Plumes
Fan you into dispaire: Haue the power still
To banish your Defenders, till at length
Your ignorance (which findes not till it feeles,
Making but reseruation of your selues,
Still your owne Foes) deliuer you
As most abated Captiues, to some Nation
That wonne you without blowes, despising
For you the City. Thus I turne my backe;
There is a world elsewhere.

# CORIOLANUS

## Act 3, Scene 3

**Coriolanus:** You common cry of curs! whose breath I hate
As reek o'th' rotten fens, whose loves I prize
As the dead carcasses of unburied men
That do corrupt my air: I banish you!
And here remain with your uncertainty!

**Context:** Caius Martius Coriolanus, a Roman general, loathes the common people. He bravely leads Rome to victory against the Volscians, and is chosen as consul by the patricians (nobles) upon his return. Reluctantly, Coriolanus humbles himself to gain the citizens' votes, but their minds are easily turned against him. Hearing that he has lost favour, Coriolanus unleashes his contempt for the plebeians (commoners) in a vicious and deliberately insulting speech.

**Dates:** Certain references in the play text suggest that *The Tragedy of Coriolanus* was first written and performed in 1608. As with *Julius Caesar,* Shakespeare drew on the English translation of Plutarch's *Lives of the Noble Grecians and Romans*, which chronicled the life of Coriolanus. The play was originally published in the First Folio of 1623.

**Image:** *First Folio, 1623.*

*Mam.* There was a man.

*Her.* Nay, come sit downe : then on.

*Mam.* Dwelt by a Church-yard : I will tell it softly,
Yond Crickets shall not heare it.

*Her.* Come on then, and giu't me in mine eare.

*Leon.* Was hee met there ? his Traine ? *Camillo* with
him ?

*Lord.* Behind the tuft of Pines I met them, neuer
Saw I men scowre so on their way : I eyed them
Euen to their Ships.

*Leo.* How blest am I
In my iust Censure ? in my true Opinion ?
Alack, for lesser knowledge, how accurs'd,
In being so blest ? There may be in the Cup
A Spider steep'd, and one may drinke ; depart,
And yet partake no venome : (for his knowledge
Is not infected) but if one present
Th'abhor'd Ingredient to his eye, make knowne
How he hath drunke, he cracks his gorge, his sides
With violent Hefts : I haue drunke, and seene the Spider.
*Camillo* was his helpe in this, his Pandar :
There is a Plot against my Life, my Crowne ;
All's true that is mistrusted : that false Villaine,
Whom I employ'd, was pre-employ'd by him :
He ha's discouer'd my Designe, and I
Remaine a pinch'd Thing ; yea, a very Trick
For them to play at will : how came the Posternes
So easily open ?

*Lord.* By his great authority,
Which often hath no lesse preuail'd, then so,
On your command.

*Leo.* I know't too well.
Giue me the Boy, I am glad you did not nurse him :
Though he do's beare some signes of me, yet you
Haue too much blood in him.

*Her.* What is this ? Sport ?

*Leo.* Beare the Boy hence, he shall not come about her,
Away with him, and let her sport her selfe
With that shee's big-with, for 'tis *Polixenes*
Ha's made thee swell thus.

*Her.* But Il'd say he had not ;
And Ile be sworne you would beleeue my saying,
How e're you leane to th'Nay-ward.

Should a like Language vse to all degre
And mannerly distinguishment leaue o
Betwixt the Prince and Begger :) I haue
Shee's an Adultresse, I haue said with w
More ; shee's a Traytor, and *Camillo* is
A Federarie with her, and one that knov
What she should shame to know her se
But with her most vild Principall : that
A Bed-swaruer, euen as bad as those
That Vulgars giue bold'st Titles ; I, and
To this their late escape.

*Her.* No (by my life)
Priuy to none of this : how will this gri
When you shall come to clearer knowle
You thus haue publish'd me ? Gentle m
You scarce can right me throughly, the
You did mistake.

*Leo.* No : if I mistake
In those Foundations which I build vpc
The Centre is not bigge enough to bea
A Schoole-Boyes Top. Away with her
He who shall speake for her, is a farre-o
But that he speakes.

*Her.* There's some ill Planet raigne
I must be patient, till the Heauens look
With an aspect more fauorable. Good
I am not prone to weeping (as our Sex
Commonly are) the want of which vai
Perchance shall dry your pitties : but I
That honorable Griefe lodg'd here, wh
Worse then Teares drowne : 'beseech y
With thoughts so qualified, as your Ch
Shall best instruct you, measure me ; an
The Kings will be perform'd.

*Leo.* Shall I be heard ?

*Her.* Who is't that goes with me ? 'bese
My Women may be with me, for you
My plight requires it. Doe not weepe(
There is no cause : When you shall knov
Ha's deseru'd Prison, then abound in T
As I come out ; this Action I now goe
Is for my better grace. Adieu (my Lor
I neuer wish'd to see you sorry, now

# THE WINTER'S TALE

## Act 2, Scene 1

**Leontes:**       How blest am I
In my just censure! in my true opinion!
Alack, for lesser knowledge! how accurs'd
In being so blest! There may be in the cup
A spider steep'd, and one may drink, depart,
And yet partake no venom (for his knowledge
Is not infected); but if one present
Th'abhorr'd ingredient to his eye, make known
How he hath drunk, he cracks his gorge, his sides,
With violent hefts. I have drunk, and seen the spider.

**Context:** Polixenes, King of Bohemia, has enjoyed a lengthy stay at the court of his childhood friend Leontes, King of Sicily, and his wife, Queen Hermione. When the time comes for Polixenes to leave, Leontes tasks Hermione with persuading him to stay. She succeeds, but Leontes becomes convinced the two are lovers. In this speech he reveals his irrational jealousy and hysterical fear of cuckoldry.

**Dates:** A performance of *The Winter's Tale* was first recorded in May 1611, when the astrologer Simon Forman saw it staged at the Globe Theatre. The play was probably written and performed earlier than this, in 1609 or 1610, and was originally published in the First Folio of 1623.

Vnder thele windowes, White and Azure lac'd
With Blew of Heauens owne tinct. But my defigne.
To note the Chamber, I will write all downe,
Such, and fuch pictures: There the window, fuch
Th'adornement of her Bed; the Arras, Figures,
Why fuch, and fuch: and the Contents o'th'Story.
Ah, but fome naturall notes about her Body,
Aboue ten thoufand meaner Moueables
Would teftifie, t'enrich mine Inuentorie.
O fleepe, thou Ape of death, lye dull vpon her,
And be her Senfe but as a Monument,
Thus in a Chappell lying. Come off, come off;
As flippery as the Gordian-knot was hard.
'Tis mine, and this will witneffe outwardly,
As ftrongly as the Confcience do's within:
To'th'madding of her Lord. On her left breft
A mole Cinque-fpotted: Like the Crimfon drops
I'th'bottome of a Cowflippe. Heere's a Voucher,
Stronger then euer Law could make; this Secret
Will force him thinke I haue pick'd the lock, and t'ane
The treafure of her Honour. No more: to what end?
Why fhould I write this downe, that's riueted,
Screw'd to my memorie. She hath bin reading late,
The Tale of *Tereus*, heere the leaffe's turn'd downe
Where *Philomele* gaue vp. I haue enough,
To'th'Truncke againe, and fhut the fpring of it.
Swift, fwift, you Dragons of the night, that dawning
May beare the Rauens eye: I lodge in feare,
Though this a heauenly Angell: hell is heere.

          *Clacke ftrikes*
            *Exit.*
One, two, three: time, time.

# CYMBELINE

## Act 2, Scene 2

**Iachimo:**        On her left breast
A mole cinque-spotted: like the crimson drops
I'th' bottom of a cowslip. Here's a voucher,
Stronger than ever law could make; this secret
Will force him think I have pick'd the lock, and ta'en
The treasure of her honour.

**Context:** Posthumus has been banished from Britain for marrying Imogen, daughter of King Cymbeline. Amongst friends in Rome, he boasts of his wife's chastity. Iachimo wagers that he can seduce Imogen, and smuggles himself into her bedroom in a chest. Here, he spies on her while she sleeps and commits to memory the signs with which he will persuade Posthumus that she has been unfaithful.

**Dates:** Certain stage directions suggest that *The Tragedy of Cymbeline* was written with the Blackfriars Theatre in mind; it was probably composed between 1610 and 1611. The play was originally published in the First Folio of 1623.

**Image:** *First Folio, 1623.*

and He ſerue thee.

npaſt?

ld him thee aſleepe,

nto his head.

ot.

? Thou ſcuruy patch:

im blowes,

hen that's gone,

for Ile not ſhew him

er danger :

urther, and by this

doores, and make a

nothing :

Tale : prethee ſtand

a little time

ceede.

cuſtome with him

ou maiſt braine him,

with a logge

ith a ſtake,

. Remember

ithout them

---

Any reaſon : Come on *Trinculo*, let vs ſing.

               *Sings.*

*Flout 'em, and cout 'em : and skowt 'em, and flout 'em,*
      *Thought is free.*

  *Cal.* That's not the tune.

        *Ariell plaies the tune on a Tabor and Pipe.*

  *Ste.* What is this ſame ?

  *Trin.* This is the tune of our Catch, plaid by the picture of No-body.

  *Ste.* If thou beeſt a man, ſhew thy ſelfe in thy likenes :
If thou beeſt a diuell, take't as thou liſt.

  *Trin.* O forgiue me my ſinnes.

  *Ste.* He that dies payes all debts : I defie thee ;
Mercy vpon vs.

  *Cal.* Art thou affeard ?

  *Ste.* No Monſter, not I.

  *Cal.* Be not affeard, the Iſle is full of noyſes,
Sounds, and ſweet aires, that giue delight and hurt not :
Sometimes a thouſand twangling Inſtruments
Will hum about mine eares ; and ſometime voices,
That if I then had wak'd after long ſleepe,
Will make me ſleepe againe, and then in dreaming,
The clouds methought would open, and ſhew riches
Ready to drop vpon me, that when I wak'd
I cri'de to dreame againe.

  *Ste.* This will proue a braue kingdome to me,
Where I ſhall haue my Muſicke for nothing.

  *Cal.* When *Proſpero* is deſtroy'd.

  *Ste.* That ſhall be by and by :
I remember the ſtorie.

  *Trin.* The ſound is going away,
Lets follow it, and after do our worke.

  *Ste.* Leade Monſter,
Wee'l follow : I would I could ſee this Taborer,
He layes it on.

  *Trin.* Wilt come ?
Ile follow *Stephano*.

                   *Exeunt.*
                   *Scena*

# THE TEMPEST

## Act 3, Scene 2

**Caliban:** Be not afeared. The isle is full of noises,
Sounds and sweet airs, that give delight and hurt not.
Sometimes a thousand twangling instruments
Will hum about mine ears; and sometimes voices,
That if I then had waked after long sleep,
Will make me sleep again; and then in dreaming,
The clouds, methought, would open and show riches
Ready to drop upon me, that when I waked
I cried to dream again.

**Context:** Prospero, the rightful Duke of Milan, was usurped and cast into exile by his brother Antonio and Alonso, the King of Naples. For the last twelve years he has enslaved Caliban and ruled the savage's native island home. Using powerful magic, Prospero raises a tempest and shipwrecks his enemies onto his shores. Stephano and Trinculo, Alonso's servants, plot with Caliban to murder his master, but become unsettled by mysterious music. In this passage, Caliban reassures his conspirators and reveals hidden depths of character.

**Dates:** *The Tempest* was probably written between 1610 and its first recorded performance in November 1611, when the King's Men performed it for King James I at Whitehall. The play was originally published in the First Folio of 1623.

**Image:** *First Folio, 1623.*

His Greatnesse is a ripening, nippes his roote,
And then he fals as I do. I haue ventur'd
Like little wanton Boyes that swim on bladders:
This many Summers in a Sea of Glory,
But farre beyond my depth: my high-blowne Pride
At length broke vnder me, and now ha's left me
Weary, and old with Seruice, to the mercy
Of a rude streame, that must for euer hide me.
Vaine pompe, and glory of this World, I hate ye,
I feele my heart new open'd. Oh how wretched
Is that poore man, that hangs on Princes fauours?
There is betwixt that smile we would aspire too,
That sweet Aspect of Princes, and their ruine,
More pangs, and feares then warres, or women haue;
And when he falles, he falles like Lucifer,
Neuer to hope againe.

    *Enter Cromwell, standing amazed.*

Why how now *Cromwell*?
 *Crom.* I haue no power to speake Sir.
 *Car.* What, amaz'd
At my misfortunes? Can thy Spirit wonder
A great man should decline. Nay, and you weep
I am falne indeed.
 *Crom.* How does your Grace.
 *Card.* Why well:
Neuer so truly happy, my good *Cromwell*,
I know my selfe now, and I feele within me,
A peace aboue all earthly Dignities,
A still, and quiet Conscience. The King ha's cur'd me,
I humbly thanke his Grace: and from these shoulders
These ruin'd Pillers, out of pitty, taken
A loade, would sinke a Nauy, (too much Honor.)
O 'tis a burden *Cromwel*, 'tis a burden
Too heauy for a man, that hopes for Heauen.
 *Crom.* I am glad your Grace,
Ha's made that right vse of it.

No Sun, shall euer vsher fort
Or gilde againe the Noble T
Vpon my smiles. Go get th
I am a poore falne man, vnw
To be thy Lord, and Master.
(That Sun, I pray may neuer
What, and how true thou ar
Some little memory of me, v
(I know his Noble Nature) n
Thy hopefull seruice perish t
Neglect him not; make vse n
For thine owne future safety.
 *Crom.* O my Lord,
Must I then leaue you? Mus
So good, so Noble, and so tr
Beare witnesse, all that haue r
With what a sorrow *Cromwe*.
The King shall haue my serui
For euer, and for euer shall be
 *Card. Cromwel*, I did not
In all my Miseries: But thou
(Out of thy honest truth) to p
Let's dry our eyes: And thus
And when I am forgotten, as
And sleepe in dull cold Marb
Of me, more must be heard o
Say *Wolsey*, that once trod the
And sounded all the Depths,
Found thee a way (out of his
A sure, and safe one, though
Marke but my Fall, and that
*Cromwel*, I charge thee, fling
By that sinne fell the Angels:
(The Image of his Maker )ho
Loue thy selfe last, cherish th
Corruption wins not more t

# KING HENRY VIII

## Act 3, Scene 2

**Wolsey:**         I have ventured,
Like little wanton boys that swim on bladders,
This many summers in a sea of glory,
But far beyond my depth. My high-blown pride
At length broke under me and now has left me,
Weary and old with service, to the mercy
Of a rude stream that must for ever hide me.

**Context:** Cardinal Wolsey has risen from humble origins to his place as Henry VIII's Lord Chancellor, acquiring powerful enemies along the way. In hope of thwarting Henry's plan to marry Anne Bullen (Boleyn), Wolsey writes to the Pope and asks him to deny the King his divorce from Katherine of Aragon. Wolsey's plot is uncovered by his rivals, and the King casts him aside. In this speech Wolsey muses on his fall and the uncertainty of royal favour.

**Dates:** *Henry VIII* was probably first staged on 29 June 1613 at the Globe Theatre; a cannon set off in Act One set fire to the thatched roof, ultimately destroying the playhouse. Originally performed under the title *All is True*, the play was published in the First Folio of 1623 as *The Famous History of the Life of King Henry the Eighth*. It is generally believed to have been written in collaboration with John Fletcher.

*Arc.* Shall we make worthy uses of this place
That all men hate so much?

*Pal.* How gentle Cosen?

*Arc.* Let's thinke this prison, holy sanctuary,
To keepe us from corruption of worse men,
We are young and yet desire the waies of honour,
That liberty and common Conversation
The poyson of pure spirits; might like women
Wooe us to wander from. What worthy blessing
Can be but our Imaginations
May make it ours? And heere being thus together,
We are an endles mine to one another;
We are one anothers wife, ever begetting
New birthes of love; we are father, friends, acquaintance,
We are in one another, Families,
I am your heire, and you are mine: This place
Is our Inheritance: no hard Oppressour
Dare take this from us; here with a little patience
We shall live long, and loving: No surfeits seeke us :
The hand of war hurts none here, nor the Seas
Swallow their youth: were we at liberty,
A wife might part us lawfully, or busines,
Quarrels consume us, Envy of ill men
Crave our acquaintance, I might sicken Cosen,
Where you should never know it, and so perish
Without your noble hand to close mine eies,
Or praiers to the gods; a thousand chaunces
Were we from hence, would seaver us.

*Pal.*

# THE TWO NOBLE KINSMEN
## Act 2, Scene 2

**Arcite:**              And here being thus together,
We are an endless mine to one another;
We are one another's wife, ever begetting
New births of love; we are father, friends, acquaintance,
We are, in one another, families;
I am your heir and you are mine.

**Context:** On the morning of his wedding to Hippolyta, Duke Theseus of Athens is forced to declare war against the cruel King Creon of Thebes. Creon's nephews, Arcite and Palamon, hate their uncle but feel duty-bound to defend their city against the Athenians. They are defeated and imprisoned but, as Arcite explains, will keep their spirits high as long as they have one another.

**Dates:** *The Two Noble Kinsmen* was based on 'The Knight's Tale', a popular story from Geoffrey Chaucer's fourteenth-century *Canterbury Tales*. Written in partnership with John Fletcher, this was Shakespeare's last play. Although first performed in 1613, it was omitted from the First Folio and was not published until 1634.

Hannah Manktelow is a doctoral researcher at the University of Nottingham and the British Library studying Shakespeare performance in the English provinces from 1769 onwards.

First published in 2016 by
The British Library
96 Euston Road
London NW1 2DB

Cataloguing in publication data

A catalogue record for this book is available from the British Library

ISBN 978 0 7123 5633 6

Text © Hannah Manktelow 2016
Illustrations © The British Library Board 2016
Designed and typeset by Rawshock Design
Printed in Malta by Gutenberg Press